teach
yourself

new clait

mac bride

teach®
yourself

new clait
mac bride

for over 60 years, more than 40
million people have learnt over
750 subjects the **teach yourself**
way, with impressive results.

be where you want to be with
teach yourself

For UK orders: please contact Bookpoint Ltd., 130 Milton Park, Abingdon, Oxon OX14 4SB. Telephone: +44 (0)/1235 827720. Fax: +44 (0)/1235 400454. Lines are open 09.00–18.00, Monday to Saturday, with a 24-hour message answering service. You can also order through our website www.madaboutbooks.co.uk.

For USA order enquiries: please contact McGraw-Hill Customer Services, PO Box 545, Blacklick, OH 43004-0545, USA. Telephone: 1-800-722-4726. Fax: 1-614-755-5645.

For Canada order enquiries: please contact McGraw-Hill Ryerson Ltd., 300 Water St, Whitby, Ontario L1N 9B6, Canada. Telephone: 905 430 5000. Fax: 905 430 5020.

Long renowned as the authoritative source for self-guided learning – with more than 30 million copies sold worldwide – the *Teach Yourself* series includes over 300 titles in the fields of languages, crafts, hobbies, business, computing and education.

British Library Cataloguing in Publication Data
A catalogue record for this title is available from The British Library.

Library of Congress Catalog Card Number: On file.

First published in UK 2003 by Hodder Headline Plc., 338 Euston Road, London, NW1 3BH.

First published in US 2003 by Contemporary Books, A Division of The McGraw-Hill Companies, 1 Prudential Plaza, 130 East Randolph Street, Chicago, Illinois 60601 USA.

Typeset by MacDesign, Southampton
Printed in Great Britain for Hodder & Stoughton Educational, a division of Hodder Headline Plc, 338 Euston Road, London NW1 3BH by Cox & Wyman Ltd., Reading, Berkshire.

Impression number   10 9 8 7 6 5 4 3 2 1
Year   2007 2006 2005 2004 2003

contents

preface

New CLAIT was introduced in September 2001 by OCR (the Oxford, Cambridge and RSA Examinations group). It was developed from the long-running and very successful RSA CLAIT (Computer Literacy and Information Technology) qualification. Over 2 million people achieved that award. OCR hopes that the revised qualification will prove to be just as successful.

This book covers the syllabus for New CLAIT Level 1 as fully as possible, given its size. It is expected that readers will be enrolled, or will later enrol, on a CLAIT course and so have access to the necessary hardware and software, practice materials for the assessments and, of course, a tutor's guidance.

To achieve the New CLAIT qualification, you must pass the first unit, *Using a computer*, and any four others. Nine out of the ten optional units are covered in this book. Each element of the unit is introduced with worked examples, and at the end of each section is an exercise and a summary of the key points that you should have learnt. For the tenth unit, *BBC Becoming Webwise*, contact your local college or go to the BBC website at **www.bbc.co.uk/becomingwebwise**.

New CLAIT concentrates on the practical essentials and the core concepts behind today's technologies. Achieving its qualification will give you a good foundation in IT. I hope that you enjoy getting there. Good luck.

Mac Bride

Spring 2003

01

using a computer

In this chapter you will learn

- about the components of a computer
- how to find, open and manage files
- how to type text
- how to print a document

1.1 Key concepts

Computer systems

Computer systems come in a wide range of shapes and sizes, from room-sized *mainframes* down to pocket-sized *hand-helds*; and are designed for an ever-widening range of purposes, from managing the accounts of global organizations to controlling production-line robots. All computer systems have certain things in common: there will be one or more processors which can understand instructions (written in the appropriate computer language); a means of getting instructions into the system and of storing them; and some form of output, which may be a display on screen or paper, or may take the form of actual work.

In the New CLAIT course, and in this book, the focus is on the PC (personal computer) – either a desktop or laptop model – running some form of Windows. For the last ten years, and for the foreseeable future, these have been and will be the standard computers – the ones that you will see on the desks in any office and in homes.

Which Windows? Which applications?

At the time of writing, there are five editions of Windows in common use – 98, Me, NT, 2000 and XP. This book draws most of its illustrations and examples from Windows 98, the edition that is currently most widely used in colleges and training organizations. For the most part, the other Windows versions look and work much the same, and where there are distinct differences, these are pointed out.

For the applications, the examples and illustrations are all drawn from Microsoft Office, the standard business application suite. I have concentrated on Office 2000, the most-used edition of the software. At the level of this book, Office 97 is identical, so the screenshots for 2000 still apply. Office XP has a different colour scheme and style of buttons, but if you look past that, it varies very little from 2000. In those few situations where it is significantly different, I have included additional material.

Hardware

It's *hardware* if it hurts when you drop it on your foot! The term refers to the physical parts of a computer system, and this includes the PC itself – the box that contains the processor, memory, disk drives, power supply, etc. plus the monitor, keyboard and mouse – and any printers, scanners, modems or other *peripherals* that may be attached to it.

Software

The term *software* covers any and every type of *program* – the sets of instructions that bring the metal, plastic, glass and silicon of the hardware to life.

There are two distinct types of software:

* Applications are what make computers useful! They include word processors, spreadsheet and database programs, games, Web browsers and e-mail software and much, much more.

* An *operating system* is a package of programs that control the hardware – it tells the PC how to send information to the screen to create images, how to move data from one part of the system to another, how to store it on disks and similar low-level chores. The operating system is the interface between the applications and the hardware. It knows how to deal with different types of monitors, drives and other components, so that – no matter who manufactured the parts or what their specifications – if the computer has Windows 98 installed, it can run any Windows 98 application. (The advantage of this is more obvious when you realize that until 20 years ago, applications were written to suit specific computers, and had to be rewritten to transfer them to a different machine.) Other examples of operating systems currently in use are Windows XP and 2000 (and other, earlier versions), Unix and Linux.

Bits and bytes

The basic unit of data – the point from which it all starts – is the *bit* (*bi*nary dig*it*). A bit can be 0 or 1, represented in the computer as *on* or *off* electric charges or magnetic states. Which means that you can't do much with one bit, but start to use them in numbers, and things get more interesting.

Eight bits together form a *byte*, which can hold any value from 0 to 255, and can represent a character or serve another purpose, such as controlling the brightness of a colour. Put bytes together and you can do much more.

Bytes can be grouped into sets of two, four or more to hold a much wider range of values – from the microscopic to the astronomical, and to the umpteenth degree of accuracy. Put a few hundred thousand together, representing characters, and you've got the text of a book (though authors will argue there's a bit more to it than that!). Use three bytes together to control the brightness of the red, green and blue elements that combine to form each pixel (dot) on screen, and you have a full-colour palette. Multiply that by a million or so, and you have a high-resolution screen. And millions pose no problems for PCs. At the time of writing, the current bog-standard, entry-level PC is capable of performing around 1,500 million operations a second!!

1,024 bytes make 1 *kilobyte* (Kb) – in computing, standard numbers are typically a multiple of 2, and $1,024 = 2^{10} = 2 \times 2 \times 2 \times 2 \times 2 \times 2 \times 2 \times 2 \times 2 \times 2$. Kilobytes are often a convenient way to express file sizes. The text for this chapter is around 50Kb.

1,024 kilobytes make 1 *megabyte* (Mb). Megabytes are typically used to describe large files or the amount of RAM memory on a PC. When this book is finished it will be output as a PostScript file for the printers, and that file will probably be around 200Mb.

1,024 megabytes make 1 *gigabyte* (Gb). This is an awful lot of data. Gigabytes are mainly used for describing the size of hard disks – a typical home PC has 40Gb of hard disk space, and will probably still not be even half full after several years' regular use.

Files

A file is a set of data held in the PC's memory or stored on a disk. Files can be grouped into two broad categories:

* *Document files* are those that hold the data produced within an application. Examples include a letter, report or story written in a word processor; a budget created in a spreadsheet, and an image drawn in a graphics program. You can reopen, edit and resave your document files as often as you like; and when you are finished with them they can be deleted, or moved to another part of the system for long-term storage.

Documents and files

In Windows and Microsoft applications, document files are normally referred to simply as *documents*.

◆ *Program files* are those which form part of applications or the operating system. A simple program may consist of a single file, but most will have a main file with a whole raft of others which provide additional or optional features. You should never mess with program files in any way. When an application is installed, its setup routine will store all the files it needs in the places it expects to find them. If you edit, move or delete a program file, the application will either not work as it should or not work at all.

The nature of a file can be identified by a three-letter extension after the main part of its name. For example, *doc* shows that the file is a Word document; *xls* identifies an Excel spreadsheet; *bmp* is a bitmap image; exe is an executable file (a program). If My Computer does not show the extensions, they can be turned on in the Folder Options – use **View > Folder Options...** to open the dialog box.

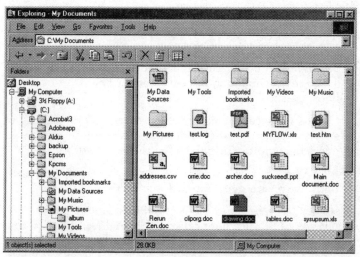

Figure 1.1 Note the extensions on the filenames – Windows uses these to identify the type of file and give it the appropriate icon. In the folder list, on the left, ⊞ shows that a folder contains subfolders.

Folders

Hard disks are huge and files rapidly build up if space is available – a quick check of this PC tells me that in just over two years, I've created or acquired around 5,000 document files, plus 35,000 program files (and I'm good about chucking away stuff that I no longer use).

Storage must be organized if you are ever to find anything! The solution is *folders* (sometimes also called *directories*). A folder is an 'elastic-sided' division of a disk. There is no limit to the number or size of files that can be stored in a folder, though the more there are, the harder it is to see the one you want. Folders may contain subfolders, which may contain their own subfolders, which may contain their own subsubfolders, *ad infinitum*.

You will learn how to create folders and organize files in section 1.5.

1.2 The PC

PC systems vary immensely, but follow a common pattern. You should normally find these components:

◆ *Monitor* or *VDU* (Visual Display Unit) – on most desktop PCs this is very similar to a standard TV, though flat LCD screens are becoming increasingly common.

◆ *System unit* – the box containing the 'works'. This may act as a base for the monitor, or stand upright beside it or on the floor beneath.

On the front you should be able to see a floppy disk drive and, normally, a CD-ROM drive, and two button switches – one is the on/off switch, the other the reset button.

At the back you will find a number of sockets and connections, most with cables plugged into them.

Inside, and best left to the professionals, are the power supply; the CD-ROM, floppy disk and hard drive; the main circuit board (the *motherboard*) containing the main processor – typically a Pentium or AMD chip – the RAM memory and other chips; plus a sound card, graphics card, modem and other circuit boards.

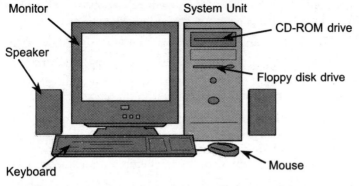

Figure 1.2 The main components of a desktop PC system.

- *Keyboard* – though mainly for entering text and numbers, the keys can also be used for controlling software, as you will see.

- *Mouse* – used for controlling the cursor on screen, allowing you to select items, start programs, draw pictures, and more.

- There will also normally be *speakers* and a *printer*, and possibly a scanner, attached.

The keyboard

Most Windows operations can be handled by the mouse, leaving the keyboard for data entry. But, keys are necessary for some jobs, and if you prefer typing to mousing, you can do most jobs from the keyboard.

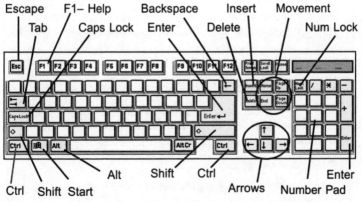

Figure 1.3 The keyboard showing the special-purpose keys.

Some operations can be run from the **function keys** – for instance, [F1] starts the Help system in any Windows application.

The **Arrow** keys can be used for moving the cursor. Above them are more movement keys, which will let you jump around in documents.

[Esc] – to escape from trouble. Use it to cancel bad choices.

[Tab] – move between objects on screen.

[Caps Lock] – put this on when you want to type a lot of capitals.

[Shift] – use it for capitals and the symbols on the number keys.

[Ctrl] or [Control] – used with other keys to make key shortcuts.

[⊞] – same as clicking **Start** on the screen.

[Alt] – used, like [Ctrl], with other keys.

[Backspace] – rubs out the character to the left of the cursor.

[Enter] – used after typing a piece of text or to start an operation.

[Delete] – deletes the character to the right of the cursor.

[Num Lock] – *on* for numbers, *off* for movement

[Backspace] and [Delete] will also delete selected files, folders and screen objects. Use with care.

Know your system

Look at your PC system. Identify the main components and any peripherals that are present. Find the PC's on/off and reset buttons, and see if the monitor has its own on/off switch.

1.3   Getting started

Routines vary, depending mainly upon the edition of Windows and whether or not you are on a network, but a startup should go along these lines.

1   Turn on the PC.

2   If the monitor has a separate switch, turn it on.

- The hard drive will whirr busily for a few moments and various messages and images will appear on screen to let you know that things are happening. It can all be safely ignored unless you are restarting after a crash.

3 If you are on a network, you will now need to *log on* – to tell the computer your user name and password.

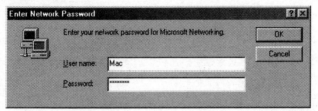

Figure 1.4 Logging on to a Windows 98 network. Passwords are never shown on screen – you only ever see a string of asterisks.

Passwords

Passwords should be easy for you to remember and hard for others to guess! They should also be changed regularly. In Windows 98, use the Passwords utility in the Control Panel to do this. In Windows XP, you will be prompted to change the password periodically, but it can be changed at any time through the User Account routine in the Control Panel.

---

4 After a few more minutes while the last files are loaded and the system is configured for your use, the Desktop will appear.

The Desktop

What do you see when you look at the screen? The answer will vary, of course, depending upon what you are doing and how you have set up the system, but some or all of these items should be visible.

Shortcuts

These are icons with links to programs, folders or places on the Internet. Clicking on the icon will run the program, open the folder or take you online. There are some shortcuts already, but you can easily add your own.

Shortcuts   Application windows   Background

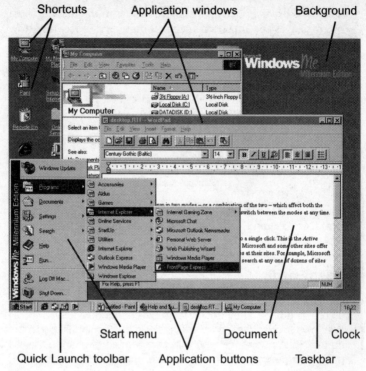

Start menu   Document   Clock

Quick Launch toolbar   Application buttons   Taskbar

Figure 1.5 The Desktop showing some of the main features. This is a Windows Me screen, but 98, NT and 2000 are very similar. Windows XP has a very different Start menu, and redesigned buttons and frames, but is still fundamentally the same.

GUIs

Windows is a **GUI** (Graphical User Interface) system. This makes it much easier to use than earlier computers which were operated by typing in commands – so you had to know what commands and options were available and type them in correctly to perform tasks. In a GUI, you can start applications or open documents by clicking on their icons, run commands by picking them from menus, select or move objects by clicking and dragging on the screen. Working with Windows is largely intuitive. If an action feels right, it probably is right – and if it isn't, you are unlikely to have done any harm as most things can be corrected easily.

Background

This may be a flat colour, a pattern, a picture or a Web page with text and images. It can be changed at any time without affecting anything else.

Application windows

When you run an application, such as My Computer, or Word, it is displayed in a window. This can be set to fill the screen or to take a smaller area so that part of the Desktop is visible beneath (see page 18).

Taskbar

This is normally along the bottom of the screen, though it can be moved elsewhere. It is the main control centre for the PC, carrying the tools to start and to switch between applications.

The **Quick Launch toolbar** gives you instant access to selected applications. The default tools run Internet Explorer, Outlook Express and Media Player. The fourth tool, Show Desktop, shrinks all open applications down to Taskbar buttons.

The **Clock** is normally also found on the Taskbar. You should find that it keeps excellent time – it even adjusts itself at the start and end of Summer Time!

When you run an application, a button is added to the Taskbar. Clicking on it will bring that application to the top of your Desktop.

Start menu

Clicking on the **Start** button opens the Start menu. Any application on your system can be run from here. The menu also leads to recently-used documents, favourite places on the Internet, the Help system and other utilities.

To start a program from the Start menu:

1 Click the **Start** button to open the menu.

2 Point to **Programs** (**All Programs** in Windows XP).

3 If necessary, point to the group name to open the submenu.

4 Click on the program's name.

Figure 1.6 A Start menu in Windows 98.

Some programs have entries on the main menu...

...others are on submenus

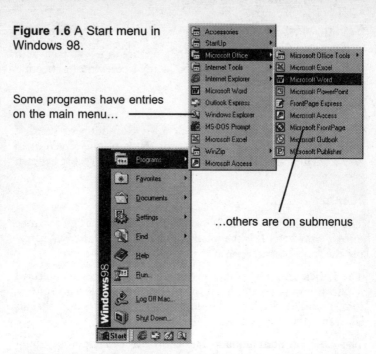

In Windows Me, the Start menu is a *smart* menu. It notes which programs you use and hides away those that you don't use. If and when you do need to get to them, the menu can be opened out fully.

In Windows XP the initial Start menu includes links to the programs and documents that you are most likely to want – Internet tools and favourite programs, recent documents, the main document folder and key utilities – with all other applications reached through the All Programs menu.

1.4 Windows techniques

Basic windows concepts

A window is a framed area of the screen that is controlled independently of any other windows. All applications are displayed in windows. If an application can handle multiple documents, each document is displayed in its own window.

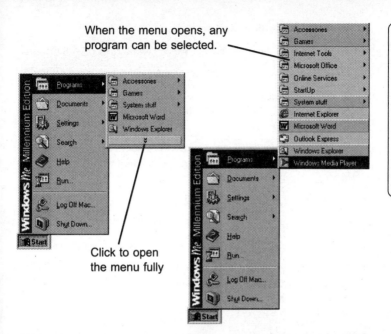

When the menu opens, any program can be selected.

Click to open the menu fully

Figure 1.7 A Start menu in Windows Me – hiding unused links makes it much simpler to reach your favourite programs.

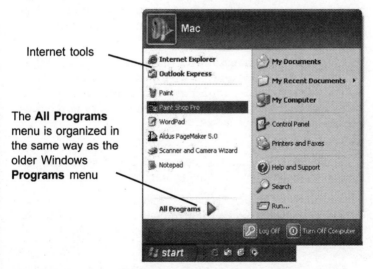

Internet tools

The **All Programs** menu is organized in the same way as the older Windows **Programs** menu

Figure 1.8 The Windows XP Start menu also adjusts to your usage, adding to the display the programs you use most often.

All windows have these features:

- **Title bar** showing the name of the application or document;

- **Minimize, Maximize/Restore** and **Close** buttons for changing the mode (see below) and for shutting down;

- An icon at the far left of the title bar leading to the window's **Control menu** (page 15);

- **Scroll bars** along the right and bottom for moving the contents within the frame, if they are wider or longer that the frame.

- A thin outer **border** for changing the size (see page 18).

Application windows also have:

- The **Menu bar**, giving access to the full set of commands;

- One or more **toolbars** containing icons that call up the more commonly-used commands. Toolbars are normally along the top of the working area, but may be down either side, or as 'floating' panels anywhere on screen.

- The **Status bar** displaying a variety of information about the current activity in the application.

Both application and document windows can be in one of three modes, and the simplest way to switch them is with the buttons at the top right:

Maximize – When maximized, an application window fills the screen and loses its frame. When a document is maximized, its title bar is merged with the application title bar and its window control buttons are placed on the far right of the Menu bar.

Minimize – an application is then visible only as a button on the Taskbar. A minimized document is reduced so that only the title bar and window mode buttons are visible.

Restore – the window is smaller than the full screen or working area. Its size can be adjusted, and it can be moved to any position on the screen. **Restore** replaces **Maximize** when the window is maximized and **Minimize** when it is minimized.

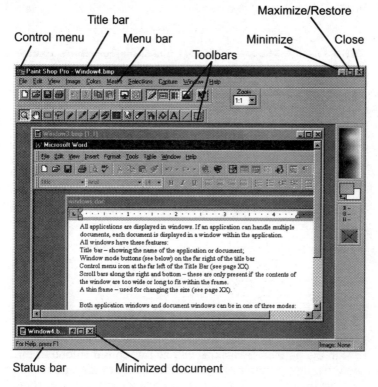

Control menu / Title bar / Menu bar / Maximize/Restore / Minimize / Close / Toolbars

Status bar   Minimized document

Figure 1.9 The main features of windows.

The Control menu

This can be opened by clicking the icon at the far left of the Title bar. But this is really here for keyboard users. Press [**Alt**] and the [**Space bar**] to open the menu in applications, or [**Alt**] and the [**Minus**] key in documents.

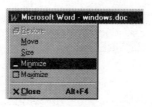

You can now Minimize, Maximize/Restore or Close using the keys. (Notice that [**Alt**] + [**F4**] is shown as a shortcut for **Close**. If a menu command has a shortcut – a combination of keys – they are shown after the command name.)

This is also where keyboard users start to Move (page 20) or change the Size (page 19) of the window.

The scroll bars

When you are working on a large picture or a long document, only the part that you are working on is displayed within the window. Scroll bars will be present along the bottom and/or right of the frame and can be used to bring the hidden parts of the document into view.

- Click on the arrows at the ends to nudge the contents in the direction of the arrow – typically a line or so at a time.

- Click on the bar to the side of or above or below the slider for a larger movement – typically just less than the height or width of the working area.

- Drag the slider. This is the quickest way to scroll through a large document.

Small movement   Slider – drag as needed

Large movement

Screen layouts

Windows allows you enormous flexibility in your screen layouts, though the simplest layout that will do the job is usually the best. You can only ever work on one application at a time – though you can copy or move files or data between two windows and there may be continuing activities, such as printing or downloading, going on in other windows. If you do not actually need to see what is happening in the other windows, the simplest layout is to run all applications in Maximized mode. The one that you are working on will fill the screen, obscuring the others, but you can easily bring one of those to the front by clicking on its button in the Taskbar.

Multiple window layouts

Sometimes you will want to be able to see two or more windows at the same time – perhaps to copy material from one application to another or to copy or move files. The simplest approach here is to use the **Cascade** and **Tile** commands. They will take all windows currently open in Maximized or Restore mode and arrange them overlapping (**Cascade**), side-by-side (**Tile Horizontally**) or one above the other (**Tile Vertically**).

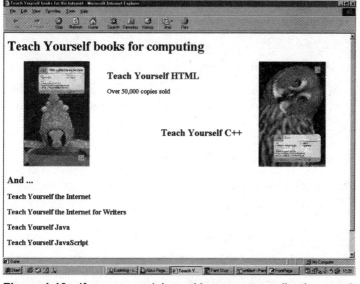

Figure 1.10 If you are mainly working on one application, run it in a Maximized window for the largest working/viewing area. Other windows can be reached, if needed, through their Taskbar buttons.

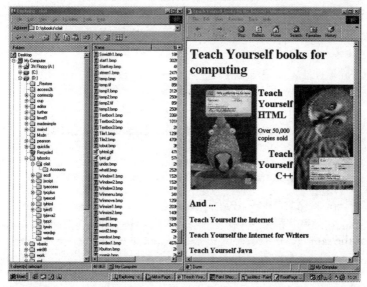

Figure 1.11 The Tile displays work better with bigger screens. A 800×600 can cope comfortably with two windows, but not more.

- Check that all the windows you want to include in the display are in Maximized or Restore mode.

- Right-click on a blank area of the Taskbar.

- Select the **Cascade** or **Tile Horizontally/Vertically** command.

- When you want to return to the previous layout, right-click the Taskbar again. The menu will now have an **Undo Cascade** or **Undo Tile** command.

Tabbing between windows

Switching between windows by using their Taskbar buttons is not always convenient. However, there are a couple of neat alternatives. Try this:

1 Hold down the [**Alt**] key and press [**Tab**]. This panel appears.

2 Press [**Tab**] again until the application that you want is highlighted – if you go off the end, it cycles back to the start.

3 Release the [**Alt**] key.

You can also hold down [**Alt**] and press [**Escape**] to switch between windows. Repeat until the one you want is at the front.

The Windows key and the Taskbar buttons

If you don't want to or cannot use the mouse to click the Taskbar buttons, hold down the [**Windows**] key and press [**Tab**]. This will select one of the Taskbar buttons – keep pressing [**Tab**] to move between the buttons. When the one you want is selected, press [**Enter**] to activate its window.

Adjusting the window size

When a window is in Restore mode, its size can be adjusted freely. This can be done easily with the mouse or with the keyboard.

Using the mouse

1 Select the document or application window.

2 Point to an edge or corner of the frame – when you are in a suitable place the cursor changes to a double-headed arrow.

3 Hold down the left mouse button and drag the edge or corner to change the window size. If you have turned on the **Show windows contents while dragging** option (on the **Effects** tab of the **Display Properties** dialog box), the window will change size as you drag. If the option is off, you will see a shaded outline showing the new window size.

4 Release the mouse button.

5 Repeat on other edges or corners if necessary.

Using the keyboard

1 Open the Control menu by pressing [**Alt**] + [**Space bar**] (application) or [**Alt**] + [**Minus**] (document).

2 Press [**S**] to select Size.

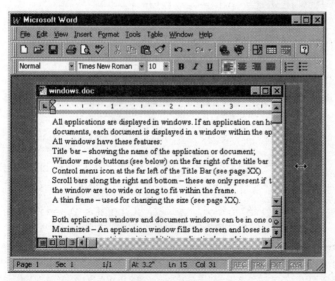

Figure 1.12 Adjusting the size of a document window. An outline shows the new size as the *Show windows contents while dragging* option has been turned off on this system.

3 Press the arrow key corresponding to the edge that you want to move. A double-headed arrow will appear.

4 Use the arrow keys to move the edge into its new position.

5 Press [**Enter**] to fix the new size.

6 Repeat for other edges or corners if necessary.

Moving windows

A window in Restore mode can be moved to anywhere on – or part-ways off – the screen (or the working area in an application). The Title bar is the 'handle' for movement.

Moving with the mouse

◆ Click on the Title bar and drag the window into its new place.

Moving with the keyboard

1 Open the Control menu and select **Move**.

2 Use the arrow keys to move the window as required.

3 Press [**Enter**] to fix the new position.

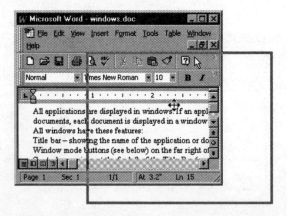

Figure 1.13 Moving a window. The 4-way arrow only appears when you start from Move in the Control menu. If *Show windows contents while dragging* is turned off, only the outline moves while you drag.

1.5 Files and folders

My Computer/Windows Explorer

My Computer and Windows Explorer are aspects of the same program (and Internet Explorer is another variation of it). They look a bit different in their default settings, and have slightly different selections of tools, but are otherwise the same.

My Computer can only be started from the **Desktop** icon. It is Windows Explorer at its simplest, with the display set to show the contents of one drive or folder.

Windows Explorer gives you easier ways to switch from one folder to another, and to move files between folders.

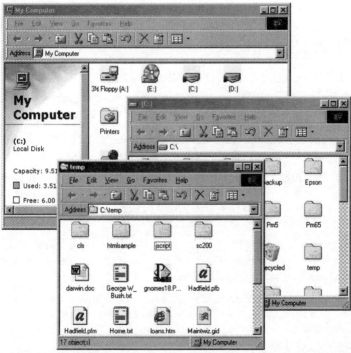

Figure 1.14 Double-click on a folder's icon to open it. A new My Computer window will open to display the folder's contents. Multiple windows can be useful for moving files between folders, but if the screen gets too cluttered, close the windows that you don't need.

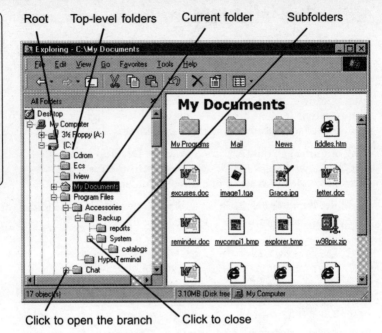

Root   Top-level folders   Current folder   Subfolders

Click to open the branch   Click to close

Figure 1.15 Windows Explorer, showing the main features. Yours may look different as there are many display options.

* Run it from the **Start** button – you will find it either in the main **Programs** menu or in the **Accessories** submenu.

The Explorer window has two panels. The left panel (the **Explorer Bar**) normally shows **Folders**, but can be used for other things or closed if not wanted (see page 23). The right panel shows the files and folders in the currently selected folder.

In the folder display, ⊞ to the left shows that a folder has subfolders. Click this to open up the branch. The icon changes to ⊟ and clicking this will close the branch.

When a folder is selected 📁, its files and subfolders are listed in the main pane. Files can be listed by name, type, date or size, and displayed as thumbnails or large or small icons, with or without details (see page 24).

The **Status bar** at the bottom shows the number of objects in the folder and the amount of memory they use, or the size of a selected file.

The controls

These are at the top of the window. The **Menu bar** is always visible. As with any Windows application, the full command set can be reached through the menu system, but those that you will use most often can be accessed faster through toolbar buttons or keyboard shortcuts.

The available menu options vary when a file, folder or drive is selected.

There are four toolbars, all of which are optional – turn them on or off through the **View** menu.

The **Standard toolbar** contains buttons for all essential jobs.

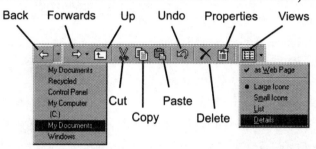

Figure 1.16 The Standard toolbar. Drop-down lists from the Back and Forwards buttons provide an easy way to move between folders that you have selected earlier in the same session.

The **Address Bar** shows the current selected folder, and can be useful for navigating around the system.

Links are shortcuts to places on the Internet – yes, you can go there from within Explorer (see Chapter 9).

Radio holds the controls and links to Internet radio stations.

Explorer Bar

The Explorer Bar is normally turned off in My Computer, and used for the **Folders** display in Windows Explorer. It can also be used to display:

• the **Search** facility. Use this to search for stuff on the Internet – and in Windows for files and folders on your system.

- the **Favorites** list – quick links to selected Web sites.

- the **History** list – links to the Web sites and to the folders on your system that you have visited recently.

To change the display, open the **View** menu, point to **Explorer Bar** and select the option.

To close the Explorer Bar and free up the full window for the file display, click the **X** in its top right corner.

The Standard buttons

- **Back** and **Forward** take you to folders opened earlier – click to go a step in either direction, or pick from the drop-down lists.

- **Up** takes you up to the next level folder, or from a folder to the drive, or a drive up to My Computer.

- **Cut** deletes the selected file but keeps a copy in the Clipboard – a special area of memory in Windows.

- **Copy** copies the selected file to the Clipboard.

- **Paste** copies the file from the Clipboard into the current folder.

- **Delete** deletes the item, placing it in the Recycle Bin (page 30).

- **Undo** undoes the previous action, if possible.

- **Views** leads to a drop-down list containing the main options from the View menu.

- **Properties** opens the Properties panel for the selected item.

In Windows Me, **Cut**, **Copy** and **Paste** are replaced by:

- **Move To** which moves the selected file to a folder picked from a list at the next stage.

- **Copy To** copies the selected file to another folder.

Displaying and sorting files

Files and folders can be shown as **Large icons**, **Small icons**, **List**, **Details** or **Thumbnails** (Windows Me and XP) – make your choice from the **View** menu or from the drop-down list on the **View** button.

Large icons aren't just easier to see, they are also larger targets if you are less than accurate with the mouse!

Small icons and **List** differ only in the order – listing either across or down the screen. Both are good for selecting sets of files (see page 27).

Details gives a column display under the headings *Name, Size, Type* and *Modified*. Click a heading to sort the files in ascending order by that feature. Click a second time to sort in descending order. This display is useful for tracking down files that you were working on at a certain date (but have forgotten the names), or for finding old or large files if you need to create some space.

Thumbnails shows – if possible – a miniature image of each file. It is, of course, best for use with images, but it can be handy for Web pages and some formatted documents.

♦ Thumbnails are not an option in Windows 98 or earlier.

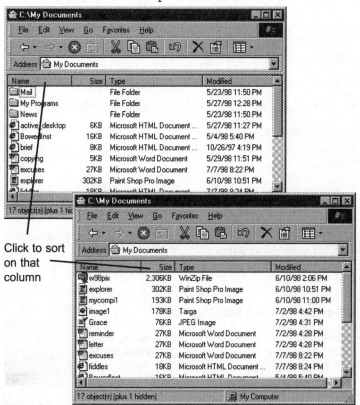

Click to sort
on that
column

Figure 1.17 The **Details** display allows you to sort the files easily.

Creating folders

Windows sets up one folder for your files, called *My Documents*. This is unlikely to be enough for very long. You need to create more folders if you will be storing more than a few dozen documents – it's hard to find stuff in crowded folders. A new folder can be created at any time, and at any point in the folder structure. Here's how:

1 In Explorer, select the folder which will contain the new one, or select the drive letter for a new top-level folder.

2 Open the **File** menu, point to **New** then select **Folder**.

3 Replace *New Folder* with a meaningful name.

♦ If you decide the folder is in the wrong place, select it and drag it into place in the All Folders list.

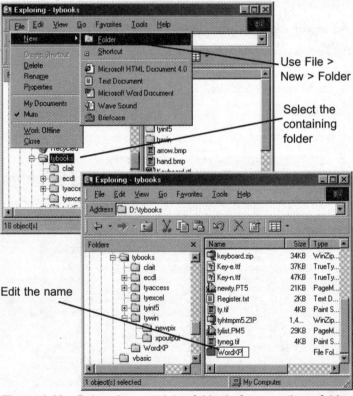

Figure 1.18 Select the containing folder before creating a folder.

Folders are files

To the PC, folders are files and can be renamed, copied and deleted just like document files.

1.6 File management

Application files – the ones that make up the software – should normally be left well alone. Start messing with these and your programs may well not work. Document files are a different matter. They must be managed actively or your folders will become cluttered, making it hard to find files.

Selecting files

Before you can do anything with any files, you must select them.

* *To select a single file*, click on it.

* *To select a set of adjacent files*, click on the window to the right of the top one and drag an outline over the set;

or select the first, hold down [**Shift**], and select the last.

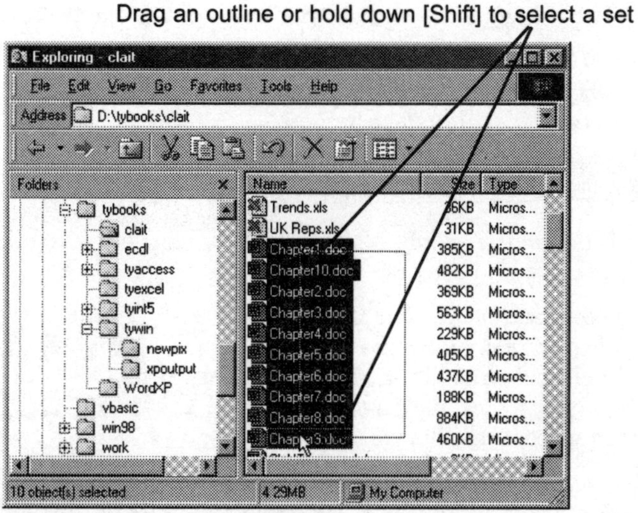

Drag an outline or hold down [Shift] to select a set

Figure 1.19 Adjacent files can be selected as a block.

- *To select scattered files*, select the first, hold down [**Control**] and select the rest in turn.

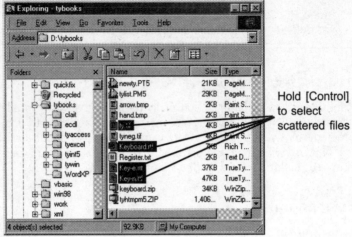

Hold [Control]
to select
scattered files

Figure 1.20 Scattered files can also be selected together.

Moving and copying files

Files are easily moved or copied. The technique is similar for both.

1 Select the file(s).

2 Scroll through the **All Folders** display and/or open subfolders, if necessary, until you can see the target folder.

3 Drag the file(s) across the screen until the target folder is highlighted, then drop it there.

- If the original and target folders are both on the same disk, this will move the selected file(s).

- If the folders are on different disks, or your target is a floppy disk, this will copy the file(s).

If you want to *move* a file from one disk to another, or *copy* within the same disk, hold down the right mouse button while you drag. When you release the button, select **Move** or **Copy** from the short menu.

Dragging is simplest in Explorer. If you are using My Computer, you can open multiple windows and drag across the screen from one to another.

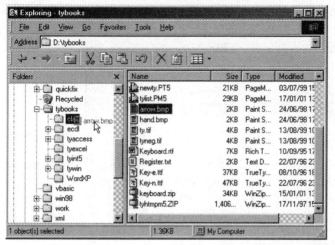

Figure 1.21 Files can be moved by dragging to their target folder.

Renaming files

If you want to edit or retype a file's name, select the file and press [**F2**], or use **Rename** from the **File** or shortcut menu. Change the name and press [**Enter**] to fix the new name.

• When renaming a file, do not change its extension! The extension tells Windows what type of file it is.

Figure 1.22 Renaming a file.

Deleting files

If a file is no longer needed, select it and press [**Delete**] or use **File > Delete**. If you delete a folder, all its files are also deleted.

Windows makes it very difficult to delete files by accident! First, you are prompted to confirm – or cancel – the deletion. Second, nothing is permanently deleted at this stage. Instead, it is transferred to the Recycle Bin.

The Recycle Bin

The true value of the Recycle Bin is only appreciated by those of us who have used systems which lack this refinement, and have spent hours – or sometimes days – replacing files deleted in error! In practice, you will rarely need this, but when you do, you will be glad that it is there! If you find that you need a deleted file, it can be restored easily.

1 Open the Recycle Bin from the Desktop icon 🗑 or from Windows Explorer (at the end of the Folders list).

2 Select the file.

3 Open the **File** menu, or right-click for the shortcut menu and select **Restore**.

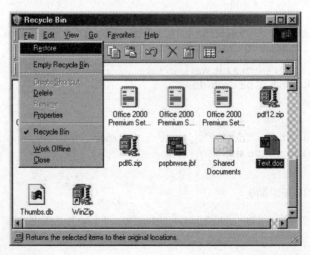

Figure 1.23 Files deleted in error can be restored from the Bin.

- If the file's folder has also been deleted, it will be re-created first, so that the file can go back where it came from.

One of the main reasons for deleting files is to free up disk space, but as long as they are in the Recycle Bin, they are still on the disk. So, make a habit of emptying the bin regularly.

- Play safe! Open the Recycle Bin and check its contents, restoring any accidental deletions, before emptying it.

1.7   Finding files

If you organize your folders and store files in the right places, you'll be able to find them immediately. However, if you are like me, you'll lose them regularly. Fortunately Windows has a neat facility for tracking down files. This looks different in Windows 98, Me and XP, though it works in the same way.

Windows 98

In Windows Explorer, open the **Tools** menu, point to **Find** and select **Files or Folders**. The Find dialog box has three tabs – use any or all of these and click **Find Now** to start the search.

Use the **Name & Location** tab if you can remember the filename, or any part of it, type it into the **Named** box. Find will look for any name that contains those characters.If you know that the file will be on a particular drive, or in a top-level folder, select this from the **Look in** drop-down list.

If you know when a file was created, modified or last accessed, use the **Date** tab. The drop-down calendar provides a very neat way to set dates!

On the **Advanced** tab you can select the type of file from the drop-down list, and/or (less usefully, I suspect) set the minimum or maximum file size.

Windows Me

In Windows Me, the Find routine has been merged with the Internet Search facility and is run in the Explorer Bar in Windows Explorer. To start it, click the ▨ icon and select **Files and Folders**.

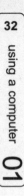

01

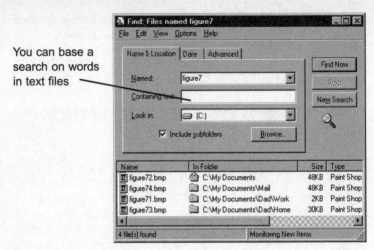

Figure 1.24 Using **Find** to track down the pictures for this chapter. The matching files are listed in a pane that appears at the bottom.

You can base a search on words in text files

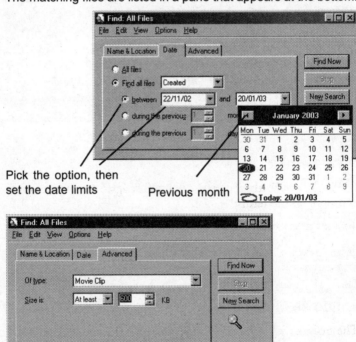

Pick the option, then set the date limits

Previous month

Figure 1.25 The Date and Advanced tabs can narrow the search.

Search lets you define a search with the same options as the Find routine. Initially, only the commonly-used search option boxes are displayed – Named, Containing text and Look in. If you want to search by Date, or Type or Size, click the Search Options >> link to open the full display. The resulting files are listed in the main pane.

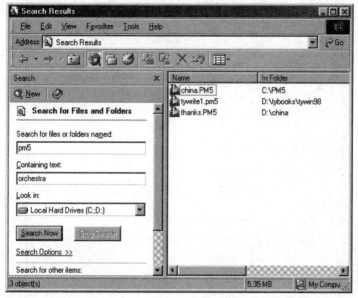

Figure 1.26 Search for Files and Folders in Windows Me.

Windows XP

In Windows XP, the Search window has again been redesigned and some of the terms changed.

To start a Search:

• Click the Search icon ⌕ Search in Explorer.

Or

• Click Start, point to Search and select For Files or Folders.

The main search option boxes – Named and Containing text – are at the top, and will normally be the only ones that are visible. The rest are reached by scrolling down the panel or by stretching the window. The Look in folder can be set here. The date options have been headed **When was it modified?** but are otherwise the same, and the advanced options are now a little more clearly labelled. A **What size is it?** setting by itself will rarely help you to find a file, but in combination with other features might prove useful – if nothing else, it will rule out files of the wrong size.

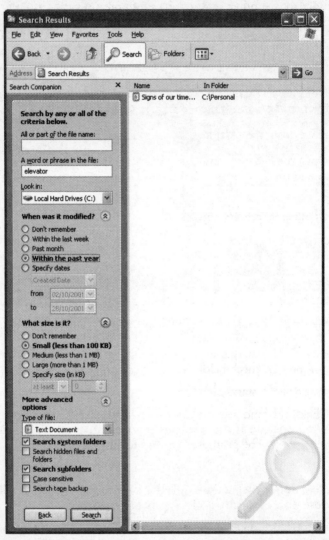

Figure 1.27 Setting Search options in Windows XP – in practice you would rarely use more than one or two of these at a time.

1.8 Shutting down

Closing windows

When you have finished with a window, close it. This will free up memory so that other applications run more smoothly, as well as reducing the clutter on your Desktop. These methods will work with any window:

♦ Click the  button in the top right corner.

♦ Hold down [Alt] and press the **minus** key to open the Control menu and select **Close**.

♦ Hold down the [Alt] key and press **F4**.

♦ Open the **File** menu and select **Exit** or **Close** to end the application.

Ending a working session

When you have finished a working session, you must log off or shut down the system – *don't just turn off your PC*. Windows runs through a shutdown routine that removes any temporary files created by the system or by applications and closes down safely.

If you simply switch off, you will find that it takes longer than usual to restart, as Windows checks – and may have to restore – essential files. It may even insist on starting in 'Safe mode' and run a thorough check before allowing you to start work.

To shut down a stand-alone PC:

1 Click **Start** and select **Shut Down** (**Turn Off Computer** in Windows XP). If any windows are open, they will be closed, and you may be prompted to save documents.

Or

Hold down [Alt] and press [F4] – if a window is open, it will close that. Press [Alt] + [F4] again to shut down.

2 Select **Shut down** (or **Turn Off**) and wait until you are told that it is safe before turning off your computer.

Or

♦ Most PCs have a **Stand By** mode which shuts down the screen and hard drive, but leaves the memory intact. In this mode, the power consumption is tiny, but the PC can be restarted readily.

♦ If you have had a crash, **Restart** will normally restore order, though on very rare occasions you may need a full shut down and power-off to recover.

To log off from a PC on a network:

1 Click **Start** and select **Log Off**.

2 Select **Log Off** at the prompt to shut any open programs, but leaves the PC running, for you or another user to use later.

Or

3 Select **Switch User** to leave your programs suspended, but let another user log in. It doesn't matter if they use the same programs as you have been using – the documents that you were working on will not be affected by anything they do. (The only possible problems you may have will occur if the other users try to work on documents that you have left open.) When they are finished you can log in again and pick up where you left off.

1.9 Health and safety

Your working area should be comfortable, safe and suitable for the job. It must also conform to the Health and Safety at Work legislation.

Things to consider when assessing whether or not the working environment is suitable for computer use include:

For *comfort*, the workstation should have:

♦ Suitable desktop space

♦ A movable keyboard, with wrist support available.

♦ If relevant, a document holder at a suitable height.

♦ An adjustable chair and sufficient desk room and leg room.

- Adequate lighting, with blinds if necessary to minimize direct sunlight on the screen.

- Flicker-free, non-glare monitors, set at, or below, eye level.

- Adequate ventilation.

- Minimized printer noise (especially with impact printers).

For *safety*, it must not have:

- Trailing cables or leads.

- Frayed power leads or worn connections.

- Overloaded power points – multiple-socket extension leads are acceptable, but multiple plugs in a single socket are hazardous.

Repetitive Strain Injury

With data entry and other jobs that involve a lot of typing or mouse use, there is a risk of RSI. A comfortable, adjustable workstation will reduce the risk, and operators should take regular breaks or changes of activity.

Security

Your computer hardware, software and its data should be protected, to reduce the risk of loss, and you need 'insurance' so that if you do suffer a loss, you can recover from it.

Hardware is the least of your problems. As long as its insured, PCs and peripherals can be replaced easily enough if they are damaged or stolen – though obviously, you should take reasonable steps to prevent this.

Software should not be too much of a problem either. If a program does become corrupted, you can usually reinstall it from its original disks or CD (which must be kept in a safe place).

Data is a different matter. It can be a crippling blow to a business to lose the records of its accounts or its clients. For home users, loss of data will rarely be a disaster, but it will be an inconvenience and some things may be irreplaceable.

Threats to your data include:

- Theft of the PC or failure of the hard drive.

- Power cuts (when unsaved data will be lost).

- Computer viruses.

- Unauthorized access to your files.

Backups

Regular *backups* – copies of data files – are your key protection.

In a business, backups may be done every few hours, at the end of the day or weekly, depending on how much files change. The norm is to run automated backups overnight when no one is working on the files. In the home, a monthly backup may be enough, with extra backups after any special documents have been created.

A backup does not have to include every data file. Normal commercial practice is to make a full backup – i.e. every file – once a week, with the daily backups only covering those files changed during that day. If a current file becomes damaged, it can be quickly restored from the lastest daily tape; if there is a major failure, then the files can be rebuilt by using the weekly backup and the daily up to the time of failure.

In large organizations, backups are usually stored on high-capacity tapes. In a small business or in the home, Zip-drives, rewritable CDs or even floppy disks should offer enough space. What is important is that the media must be removable, so that it can be stored away from the computer, and ideally in a fire-proof safe. Then if the computer is stolen or goes up in smoke, at least your data is still there.

Viruses

Viruses are programs that spread from one computer to another hidden in e-mails or attached to other software. Some viruses are merely irritating, others are very damaging, wiping entire hard disks. With those that spread by e-mail, the process of spreading is in itself damaging. Take for example, the 'love bug' virus. This appeared on its victim's PCs as an e-mail message saying 'I love you' and asking them to open the attached love letter. Opening this document, set the virus working. It erased some types of music, graphics and other files – which was bad enough – but even more damaging, it sent a copy of itself to everyone in the victim's address book. The flood of e-mails swamped many networked organizations, forcing them to close down their e-mail service until all the infected PCs had been cleaned up.

To protect your system against viruses:

* Only install software from reputable sources – and only download from trusted sites on the Internet.

* Don't open attachments in e-mail from people you don't know, and only open those from people you do know if you are expecting the attached files and know what they are.

* Install anti-virus software, to find and remove any that make it past your defences.

Keeping out unauthorized users

Passwords help to keep files safe from unauthorized users. On a local area network, users have to give their name and password to get into the system, and can normally only access files in their own folders or in those which are open to all users.

Some applications allow users to set passwords to protect individual files. These should be used if the data is confidential, or there is any danger of accidental damage to the files.

When setting a password, aim for something you can remember easily but which other people are unlikely to guess. Combinations of letters and numbers are often better than simple words – but not your car registration or your birthday, they are too obvious!

1.10   Exercise

In this activity, you are going to use Notepad. This is a simple text editor, which can be used to create plain text files – i.e. not formatted, as from a word processor (see page 46 for more on the difference between text editors and word processors). Plain text is used for e-mail, programming and for quick notes.

1   Start Notepad. Click the **Start** button, point to **Programs**, then **Accessories** and click on **Notepad**.

2   Type in some text – perhaps a few notes to remind you about the key points from this chapter.

The cursor – a flashing line – shows you where characters will appear when you type. If you want to go back and add something into the existing text, point and click with the mouse to place the cursor where you want to start typing.

3 If you make a mistake, press [**Backspace**] to erase the last character(s) that you have typed.

Click on a name to open a menu

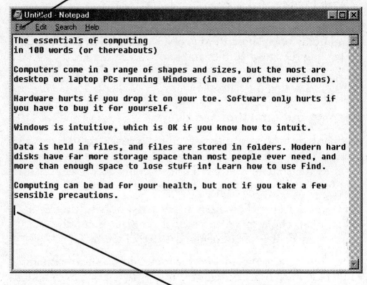

New text will appear at the cursor

Figure 1.28 Using Notepad to create a simple text file.

Saving and opening files

1 When you have done, click on **File** in the Menu bar to open the **File** menu, then click on **Save As…**

The **Save As** dialog box will open.

2 In the **Save in** box, you will see the name of the folder in which the file will be saved. If this is not where you want it to go, click the drop-down arrow to its right and select a higher-level folder or drive from there, or select a subfolder from the main display.

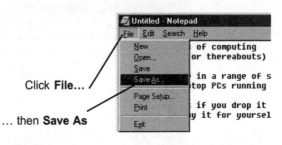

Click **File...**

... then **Save As**

3 In the **File name** box, type a name that will remind you of its subject.

4 Click the **Save** button.

We will now wipe the slate, then get the text back by opening the file.

5 Click **File** in the Menu bar then click **New**. The working area will be cleared, ready for you to start a new document.

6 Click **File** again, and then click **Open**.

Open this list to reach higher-level folders

Names can have several words

Notepad saves files as text

7 At the Open dialog box, you should find that the **Look in** folder is the one where you saved the file. If it is not, change to the right folder as in step 2. Find the file and click on it to select it, then click the **Open** button.

8 Add a few more lines of text to your document and save it again. This time, open the **File** menu and click **Save**.

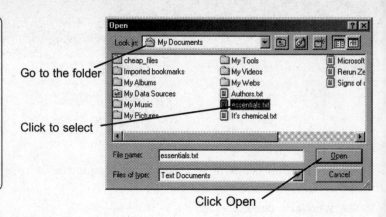

Go to the folder

Click to select

Click Open

Save and Save As

These two Save options will be found in most applications.

- Use **File > Save** when you are editing an existing file. The new version will replace the old one on the disk. Don't wait until the end of a long session before saving. Save early and save often – it only takes a moment and it ensures that the work you have done is safe if the PC crashes or someone snags the power lead or something else goes wrong.

- Use **File > Save As** when you save the file, or when you want to save a copy with a new name, so that you retain the original version of the file.

Printing

Printing from Notepad is easy – mainly because you have no control over it! Before you start make sure that your printer is turned on and has paper in it. If you are on a network, find out which printer normally handles the output from your PC.

- Click **File** to open the menu, and select **Print**.

  A message will appear to tell you that the file is being printed – but you won't have time to read it unless you are very quick or the file is very long!

Summary

*   Hardware refers to computers, printers, modems and other peripherals. A PC system normally consists of the system unit, a monitor, a keyboard and a mouse.

*   Software can be divided into two types: operating systems, such as Windows, and application programs such as Word.

*   Data is stored in files on disks, organized into folders. The size of files is measured in bytes or kilobytes.

*   Windows is a GUI system, with its main controls easily accessible through the Desktop.

*   In any application, all the commands can be reached through the menu system. The most common ones can usually also be reached through toolbar buttons.

*   All programs run inside windows. You can change the shape, position and layout of windows on the Desktop.

*   The mouse responds to single and double clicks of the left button, and to single clicks of the right button.

*   Certain keys serve specific functions.

*   The Start menu gives you quick ways to start work.

*   Windows has simple ways to set options and make choices.

*   My Computer and Windows Explorer are programs for managing files and folders. The View options allow you to set up the display to suit yourself.

*   Files can be displayed as large or small icons or thumbnails, or in a detailed list.

*   You can create new folders as and where you need them.

*   Files can be moved, copied, renamed or deleted.

*   To select sets of files, drag an outline with the mouse, or use the mouse in combination with [Shift] or [Ctrl].

*   When renaming files, do not change the extension, as this identifies the nature of the file.

- When a file is deleted, it is transferred to the Recycle Bin. If necessary, files can be restored from the Bin.

- The Find or Search routine allows you to track down files through their name, location, date, type or size.

- At the end the day you should close down properly, either by shutting down the PC or by logging off the network.

- You should be able to adjust your workstation for your comfort. Your workspace should be adequately lit and ventilated and electrically safe.

- You should adopt safe working practices to avoid viruses and to keep your files secure.

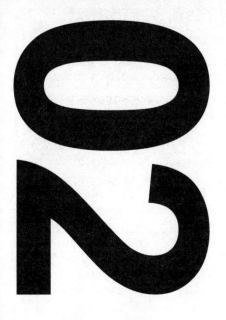

02

word processing

In this chapter you will learn

- about word processors and text editors
- how to enter and edit text
- how to change the format and font of text
- how to layout paragraphs and documents
- how to print a document

2.1 Word processors and text editors

In computing there are two types of text:

*   *Plain text* consists simply of the words and punctuation. It is used where the content is the only thing that really matters, e.g. e-mail messages and the source code of computer programs or Web pages (see Chapter 9). Plain text files are very compact, taking only one byte per character. The text of this chapter, for example, would make a file of only 24Kb.

*   *Formatted text* has had its appearance enhanced by the use of colour, different fonts and type sizes, the layout of the paragraphs and other factors. It is used where good presentation is important, or where items need to be picked out from the surrounding text, e.g. letters, brochures, reports and books. Formatting adds to the size of files. This text of this chapter, as a formatted Word document makes a file of 78Kb.

It's no surprise that there are two types of programs for producing text:

*   Text editors, such as Notepad (see page 39) are used for producing plain text files. They typically have few facilities: they will let you enter and edit text, save and open files, and may have a find and replace feature. As they are such simple programs – Notepad is just over 50Kb – they are quick to start and use very little memory when running.

*   Word processors, such as Microsoft Word, can do all that a text editor can do and far, far more. They give you control over just about every aspect of the appearance of text – its size, shape, colour, position – and of the page on which it will be printed. You can set the size and layout of the paper and add running heads, page numbers and footnotes to every page, or selected pages. Images and (formatted) data from other applications can be imported into documents; contents lists and indexes can be generated easily – useful features with large documents. Word's other facilities include spelling and grammar checkers, and even a thesaurus. All these extra facilities add greatly to the size of the program – Word is nearly 9Mb – which means that it takes longer to start, runs a little slower, and uses far more memory than a text editor.

Starting Word

Like most applications, Word can be started in several ways.

- Click the **Word** icon 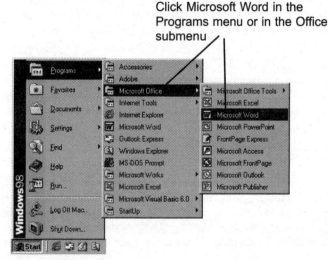 on the Desktop.
- Click the **Start** button, point to **Programs** and click **Microsoft Word** there or in the **Microsoft Office** submenu.

> Click Microsoft Word in the
> Programs menu or in the Office
> submenu

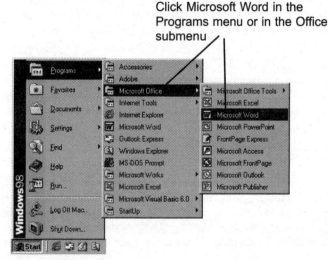

Figure 2.1 Starting Word from the Start menu.

Word's tools

All of Word's commands and options can be reached through the menu system, but most can also be selected – more conveniently – through toolbar buttons. When Word first opens, two toolbars are displayed – the Standard and Formatting. All the tools that you need on this course can be found on those toolbars, as shown in Figure 2.2.

- Start Word and find the tools labelled here. Point to each in turn and wait for the tooltip to appear. This will give its name and keyboard shortcut – if one is available.

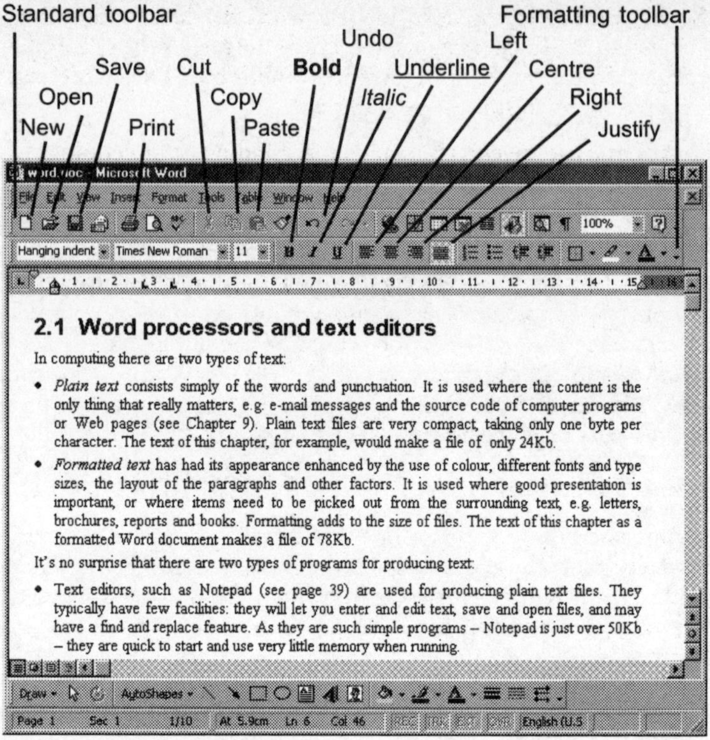
Standard toolbar
Formatting toolbar
Undo
Left
Save
Cut
Bold
Underline
Centre
Open
Copy
Italic
Right
New
Print
Paste
Justify
word.doc - Microsoft Word
File Edit View Insert Format Tools Table Window Help
100%
Hanging indent
Times New Roman
11
2.1 Word processors and text editors
In computing there are two types of text:
Plain text consists simply of the words and punctuation. It is used where the content is the only thing that really matters, e.g. e-mail messages and the source code of computer programs or Web pages (see Chapter 9). Plain text files are very compact, taking only one byte per character. The text of this chapter, for example, would make a file of only 24Kb.
Formatted text has had its appearance enhanced by the use of colour, different fonts and type sizes, the layout of the paragraphs and other factors. It is used where good presentation is important, or where items need to be picked out from the surrounding text, e.g. letters, brochures, reports and books. Formatting adds to the size of files. The text of this chapter as a formatted Word document makes a file of 78Kb.
It's no surprise that there are two types of programs for producing text:
Text editors, such as Notepad (see page 39) are used for producing plain text files. They typically have few facilities: they will let you enter and edit text, save and open files, and may have a find and replace feature. As they are such simple programs – Notepad is just over 50Kb – they are quick to start and use very little memory when running.
Draw
AutoShapes
Page 1
Sec 1
1/10
At 5.9cm
Ln 6
Col 46
English (U.S

Figure 2.2 The Microsoft Word screen, showing the main controls. Another ten toolbars are available and can be opened as needed, via the **View > Toolbars** menu.

2.2 Entering and editing text

Entering text

To create new text, type it in through the keyboard. The text will appear at the insertion point, which is marked by a flashing line. If the insertion point is not where you want it, move it into place with the arrow keys or point and click with the mouse.

Wordwrap and new lines

When you reach the right-hand side of the working area *keep typing*! Word automatically starts a new line when needed, carrying the word down to the next line if it won't fit. This is known as **wordwrap**. If you later change the size of the text or the size of the margins, so that more or fewer words will fit on a line, Word will rewrap the text to suit the new settings.

Press [**Enter**] at the end of a paragraph, heading or bullet point to force the following text to start on a new line.

Correcting errors

If you make a mistake and spot it immediately, use [**Backspace**] to rub out the character(s) that you have just typed. If you find a mistake later, click the insertion point into the text and use [**Backspace**] to rub out characters to its left, or [**Delete**] to erase to the right. You can also use either key to delete a selected block of text (see the next page for how to select text).

Insert/Overwrite

If you start typing within some existing text, the new text will normally push the old text along to make room. This is *Insert* mode. If you want the new text to replace the old, press [**Insert**] to switch to *Overwrite* mode. Press [**Insert**] again to return to Insert mode.

Overwrite is ON

Figure 2.3 The Insert/Overwrite mode indicator.

Editing text

Word processing on computers has replaced the use of typewriters for one reason above all others – when you are word processing you can edit text far more efficiently. Mistakes are easily corrected and you can copy and move blocks of text without having to retype it.

Accuracy counts

Check the text as you go, and check your spelling (page 62) at the end. In CLAIT assessments, accuracy is important.

Selecting text

Before you can do any kind of editing on a block of text, you must first select it. A 'block' can be any size, from a single character to the whole document. How you select depends upon how big a block you want.

To select with the mouse:

a word	double-click anywhere in the word
a line	click in the margin to the left of the line
a paragraph	triple-click anywhere in the paragraph
any other text	click at the start of the block and drag to the end.

To select with keys:

all the text	press [**Control**] and [**A**]
any size block	move the insertion point to the start of the block, hold down [**Shift**] and move to the end using…
Arrows	one character left or right, one line up or down
	one word left or right if [**Control**] is held down
Home	start of line; start of text with [**Control**]
End	end of line; end of text with [**Control**]
PgUp	one screenful up
PgDn	one screenful down

Cut, Copy and Paste

If you look at the Edit menu of any Windows application, you will find the commands **Cut**, **Copy** and **Paste**. You will also find them on the short menu that opens when you right-click on a selected object. These are used for copying and moving data within and between applications.

- **Copy** copies a selected block of text, picture, file or other object into a special part of memory called the *Clipboard*.

- **Cut** deletes selected data from the original application, but places a copy into the Clipboard.

- **Paste** copies the data from the Clipboard into a different place in the same application, or into a different application – as long as this can handle data in that format.

The data normally remains in the Windows Clipboard until new data is copied or cut into it, or until Windows is shut down.

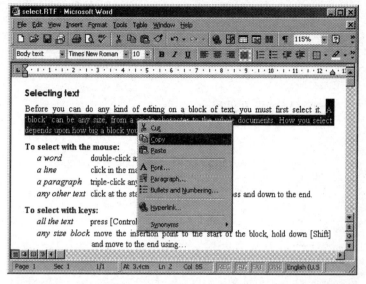

Figure 2.4 The short menu offers the quickest route to the Cut and Paste commands. If the Clipboard is empty, Paste will be 'greyed out' or omitted from the menu.

The Office Clipboard

A simple **Edit > Paste** pastes in the last item cut or copied, but Word 2000 has its own Clipboard that can hold up to 12 items. If you open the Clipboard toolbar, you can select any single item to paste, or click **Paste All** to copy all the items at once.

Drag and drop

This is an alternative to cut and paste for moving objects within an application. The technique is simple:

1 Select the block of text.
2 Point anywhere within the highlighted text.
3 Hold down the left mouse button and move the ⟍ cursor .
4 Release the button to drop the block into its new position.

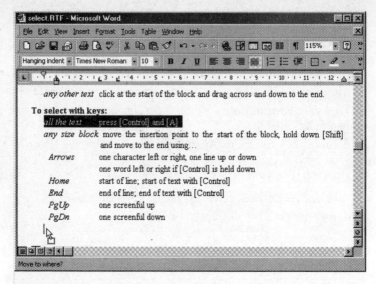

Figure 2.5 The thin bar to the left of the arrow shows where the text will go when dropped.

2.3 Find and Replace

The Find facility will locate a given word or phrase in a document. At the simplest, you just enter the text that you are looking for, and set it off. If it is a very large document, or the text alone is not enough to identify the place you want to locate, you can set other criteria to narrow down the search.

To find:

1 Open the **Edit** menu and select **Find…**
2 Enter the word or phrase.
3 Click **Find Next**.

What do you want to find?

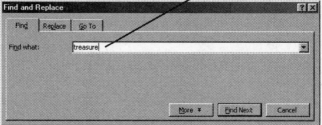

Or, if a simple search finds too many irrelevant matches:

4 Click the **More** button.

5 Set the **Search** direction, **Down** or **Up**.

6 Tick the options as required. The most useful ones are:

Match case – if looking for 'Smith', ignore 'smith' or 'SMITH'

Find whole words only – e.g.for 'now', ignore 'snow', 'known' or similar

Sounds like – use for tricky spelling. The word will be found if your guess is close enuff…

7 Click **Find Next**.

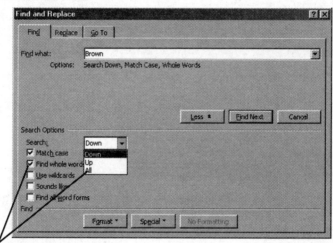

Options can focus a search

Replace

Replace is an extension of Find – the main difference is that you specify the text to insert in place of the found text. It is typically used for updating reports or work schedules, but it could be used by unscrupulous writers to create new books by changing the names of the characters and places!

1 Open the **Edit** menu and select **Replace…**

2 Enter the word or phrase to find, and the text to replace it with.

3 If you want to check each occurrence before you replace it, click **Find Next**, and when the text is found, click **Replace** (or **Find Next** to leave that occurrence).

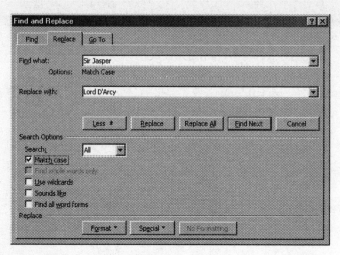

Figure 2.6 One click on **Replace All**, and my book's got a new hero!

4　If you are sure that you want to replace all occurrences, click **Replace All**.

2.4　Formatting text

You can set the typeface, size, style and colour of any amount of text, from a single character to the whole document.

Most formatting can be set using the buttons and drop-down lists in the Formatting toolbar, and can be done before or after typing in the text.

To set the formatting before you type, place the insertion point where you want the new text to go – normally at the end of any existing text – and set your formatting options. These will then be applied to everything you type until you change them. To format existing text, select it (see page 50) then set the options.

Fonts

The font, or typeface, sets the style, shape and – to some extent, the size and weight – of characters. It is therefore the most important aspect of formatting text, and the one that should normally be set before setting the size, or adding bold or other effects.

Fonts can be grouped into three categories:

- Serif fonts have little tails (or *serifs*) at the end of the strokes. This makes them easier on the eye, which is why they are often used for large blocks of text. This is Garamond. Other examples are Bookman, Times New Roman and Lucida Bright.

- Sans serif fonts have simpler lines. They are often used for captions and headings. Examples of sans serif fonts include Arial, Century Gothic and Gill Sans.

- Display fonts are those where the decorative effect or impact is more important than legibility. They are used for posters, advertisements, cards and similar. Examples include **ALGERIAN**, **Broadway** and Comic Sans.

Some fonts are naturally larger than others. All the examples above are nominally the same size (11 points), but look how much bigger Lucida Bright or Century Gothic appear than others in their sets. This is why you should always set the font before the size.

The simplest way to set the font is by using the drop-down list on the Formatting toolbar.

1 Select the text to be formatted.

2 Click the ⬇ button to the right of the font name to drop down the list.

3 Select an option from the list.

The size, highlight and text colour are set in the same way, from drop-down lists and palettes. Click the down arrow by the side of the button to display the options.

Fonts and symbols

There are also fonts like ✚✇■℔♌✚■℔✦ (Wingdings) and Σψμβολ (Symbol) which are small images that can be embedded in text, rather than characters. Explore the fonts on your PC – open the **Character Map** (in the **Accessories > System Tools** menu) and see the characters and symbols that are available in the different fonts.

Adding emphasis

If you want to add emphasis to a word or phrase, or make a heading more distinctive, you can use **bold**, *italics* or <u>underline</u>. These can all be set easily using the buttons on the Formatting toolbar.

1 Select the text to be formatted.

2 Click: the **B** button to turn **Bold** on

the *I* button to turn *Italics* on

the <u>U</u> button to turn <u>Underline</u> on.

To remove the emphasis, select the text and click the button again.

Other text formatting tools

There are three other key aspects of formatting that can be set from the toolbar buttons. These can all be applied to any amount of text, from a single character to the whole document.

- ◆ **Font size** is measured in points, and 72 points make one inch. Normal text for letters, reports, etc. should be between 10 and 12 point. This text is 11 point.
- ◆ **Highlight** gives text a coloured background. You have a limited choice of (bright) colours.
- ◆ **Text colour** – sets the colour used for the characters. Click on a colour to select it, or if there is nothing suitable, then click **More Colors…** to mix your own.

Text colour

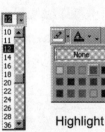

Font size   Highlight

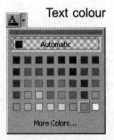

Using the Font dialog box

If you want to set several font options at the same time – perhaps to make a heading larger, bold and in a different face – or you want to set one of the less-used options, you can do it through the Font dialog box.

This approach is particularly good if you are not sure which font to use, or which settings to apply, as it has a preview pane, which shows you how the text will appear.

1 Select the text to be formatted.

2 Open the **Format** menu and select **Font...**

3 At the Font dialog box, make sure that you are on the **Font** tab.

4 Set the font, style, size and/or other options as required

5 Check the Preview and adjust the settings if necessary.

6 Click **OK**.

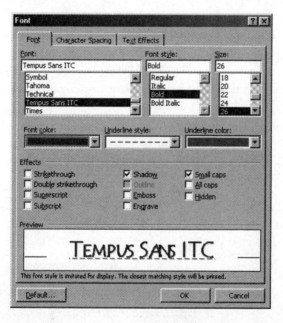

Figure 2.7 The **Font** dialog box brings together all the options from the Formatting toolbar, plus a range of special effects. The settings on the Character Spacing tab give control of the width of characters and the spacing between them; the Text Effects options can be used to highlight selected text.

2.5 Paragraph formatting

There are some formatting options that can only be applied to whole paragraphs. These control the indent and alignment of the text between the margins, and the spacing between lines and between paragraphs.

Margins

The margins are the areas around the edge of the page where text cannot be typed (except for headers and footers – see below). They are normally the same for the whole document, and are set through the Page Setup.

The main margin settings determine the distances from the page edges. The defaults are 1 inch (2.54 cm) for the top and bottom, and 1.25 inches (3.17 cm) on the left and right.

The *gutter* is extra margin to allow for stapling or binding, and can be either on the left or top of the page.

Where pages are to be printed on both sides, and then bound, the left and right-hand pages may be different. If so, turn on *Mirror margins*, then set the inside and outside margins.

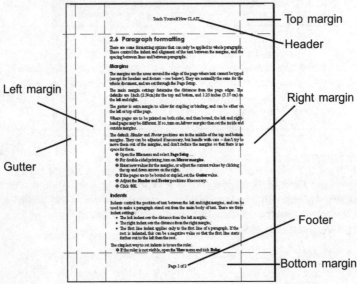

Figure 2.8 Margins and page layout.

1 Open the **File** menu and select **Page Setup…**
2 For double-sided printing, turn on **Mirror margins**.
3 Enter new values for the margins, or adjust the current values by clicking the up and down arrows on the right.
4 If the pages are to be bound or stapled, set the **Gutter** value.
5 Click **OK**.

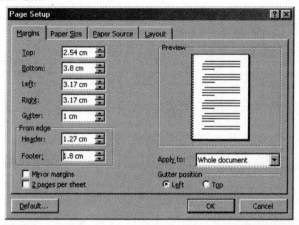

Figure 2.9 The **Page Setup** dialog box, with the settings adjusted to give a small gutter on the left, and a deeper bottom margin.

Headers and footers

These are areas within the top and bottom margins where you can place material that is to appear on every page, e.g. page numbers, the document name, or the date of printing. They are not covered at this level of New CLAIT.

Indents

Indents control the position of text between the left and right margins, and can be used to make a paragraph stand out from the main body of text. There are three indent settings:

* The left indent sets the distance from the left margin;
* The right indent sets the distance from the right margin;
* The first line indent applies only to the first line of a paragraph. If the rest is indented, this can be a negative value so

that the first line starts further out to the left than the rest. This is called a *hanging indent*, and is used for bulleted points, as here!

The simplest way to set indents is to use the ruler.

1 If the ruler is not visible, open the **View** menu and tick **Ruler**.
2 Select the text to be indented.
3 Click on the indent marker, and drag left or right as required – the dotted line will show you how it will affect the text.

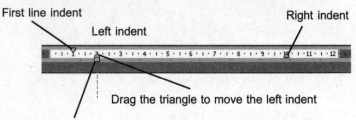

First line indent

Left indent

Right indent

Drag the triangle to move the left indent

Drag the box to move the left and first line indents together

Justification or alignment

These settings control how the text aligns with the margins – or with the indent, if they are set.

Left aligned text is flush with the left margin, but ragged on the right-hand side. Left-aligned is the default in Word. This text is left aligned.

> **Right aligned** text is flush with the right margin. A common example of its use is for the sender's address on a letter.

> Centre alignment sets each line mid-way between the margins.
> Headings are often centred.

Justified makes the text flush with both margins, for all except the last line of a paragraph. It gives a page a neater look than left alignment, but can create wide gaps between words, especially where the columns are narrow or the text contains long words. This paragraph is justified.

In Word, the simplest way to set alignment is to use the toolbar buttons.

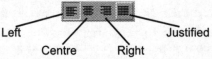

Left

Centre

Right

Justified

1   Select the paragraph(s) to be formatted.
2   Click the appropriate toolbar button.

Spacing

There are two types of spacing:

*   **Line spacing** refers to the amount of vertical space between lines of text within a paragraph. Use *1.5* to open up a paragraph and draw attention to it; *Double* spacing if you want to leave room for people to write notes on the printout.

*   **Before** and **After** refers to the spacing between paragraphs. Setting one of these to 12 point is equivalent to putting a blank line (of normal text size) between paragraphs, but thinner or wider spacing can be used as required.

If you want to separate paragraphs by a standard-width blank line, just press [**Enter**] twice after each paragraph – once to end it, and once to make an extra line.

If you want to adjust the spacing in any other way, it can only be done through the **Paragraph** dialog box.

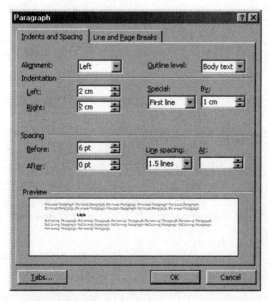

Figure 2.10 The **Paragraph** dialog box – alignment and indents can also be set from here.

1 Select the paragraph(s).

2 Open the **Format** menu and select **Paragraph...**

3 On the **Indents and Spacing** tab, open the **Line spacing:** drop-down list and select the level.

4 For spacing between paragraphs, set either the Before or After value – either enter the new value or click the little arrow buttons to nudge it up or down.

House styles and conventions

Many organizations have their own preferred way of laying out pages and formatting text. The house style may specify the fonts and sizes, the margin sizes, contents of headers and footers, etc. Some of these will be defined into templates (pre-styled blank documents) which are used to create new documents; others need your attention.

Watch out for these two widely-used conventions.

Paragraphs are normally separated by a blank line, created by an extra [**Enter**] keypress.

Some house styles call for double spaces after full stops. This was the rule when documents were produced on typewriters, but is falling out of use now that we have word processors – the extra space can create a wide gap in justified text.

Check the house style for your organization.

2.6 Spell checking

Spell checking is present in all Office applications. It uses a good dictionary, but this does not cover everything. Proper names, technical and unusual words may be unrecognized and thrown up as 'errors'. These can be added to your own dictionary, so that they are not seen as errors in future. Words spelt correctly, but used in the wrong way, e.g. 'there' when it should be 'their' are not picked up by the spell checker – but might be by the grammar checker.

Word and PowerPoint have a check-as-you-type option. You may prefer to just run a spell check after you have finished – especially if you have a lot to do and need to watch the keyboard rather than the screen!

1 If you want to check *part* of a document, or a block of cells in a spreadsheet, select it.

2 Open the **Tools** menu and select **Spelling** or click .

When a word is not recognized you can:

* Select a **Suggestion** and click **Change**.
* If it is a valid word click **Ignore**.
* Click **Add** to put it in a custom dictionary.
* Click in the **Not in Dictionary** slot, edit the word then click **Change**.

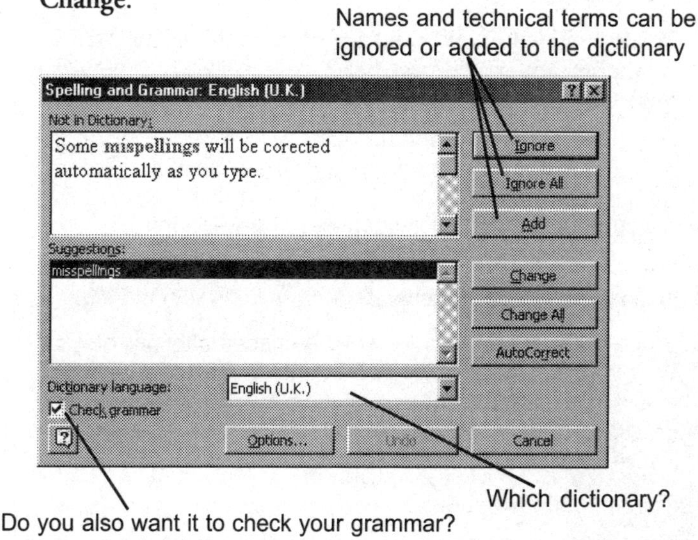

Names and technical terms can be ignored or added to the dictionary

Which dictionary?

Do you also want it to check your grammar?

Figure 2.11 Running a spell check. Accuracy counts in CLAIT, so always spell check your documents before saving or printing.

2.7 Documents and files

Saving documents

Documents should be saved regularly. If you do not save your work, it will be lost if the computer is turned off or there is a system crash.

The first time that you save the file, you need to give it a name and decide on the folder in which it will be stored. When you save it again, you will normally simply replace the existing file with a new copy – and this can be done with a single click of a button. Sometimes you will want to save the current version of the file with a new name or in a different folder, retaining the old version as a backup or for future reference.

1 Open the **File** menu and select **Save...** or **Save As...** – either way the **Save As** dialog box will appear.

2 Select the folder in which to save the document. Open the **Save in** list and select the drive, then work down to the folder as necessary.

3 A filename will have been suggested, based on the first words in the document. Edit it or replace it to give a name you will recognize and remember.

4 The **Save as type** is normally *Word Document*, but a file can be saved as a *Web page*, or as *Text*, or in a format suitable for another word processor.

5 Click **Save**.

Figure 2.12 The **Save As** dialog box – use this when you first save a file, or when you want to resave it with a new name.

To resave the file with the same name:

◆ Click 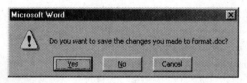 the **Save** button – that's it!

To resave the file with a new name or in a different folder/drive:

◆ Open the **File** menu and select **Save As...** then complete the dialog box as required.

Closing files

When you have finished work on a file, it should be closed. If you have edited the document and not saved the latest version, you will be prompted to do so.

1 Open the **File** menu and select **Close**.

2 If the file has been changed since the last save, you will be prompted to save it.

Click **Yes** to save, **No** to close without saving or **Cancel** to return to the open document.

Opening files

When you want to read or work on a file again, it must be opened.

To open a file:

1 Open the **File** menu and select **Open**.

2 At the **Open** dialog box, work your way through to the folder in which the file is stored.

3 If you cannot remember where the file is stored, but can remember when you last worked on it, click the **History** button and list the files in date order.

4 If the folder contains so many files that it is difficult to see the one you want, restrict the **Files of type** to *Word Documents*.

5 Click on a file to select it. If you are not sure that it is the right file, wait a moment and check it in the preview pane.

6 Click **Open**.

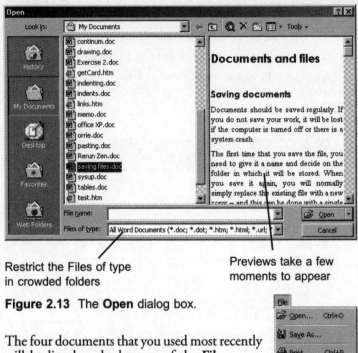

Restrict the Files of type
in crowded folders

Previews take a few
moments to appear

Figure 2.13 The **Open** dialog box.

The four documents that you used most recently
will be listed at the bottom of the **File** menu,
and can be opened by clicking on them.

2.8 Printing

To print the document with the default settings – which will
usually mean printing one copy of all the pages, at normal quality
on the printer connected to (or on a network, assigned to) your
PC – simply click 🖨 the **Print** button on the Standard toolbar.

To check or change the settings before printing:

1 If you want to print only a selected part of the document,
select it first.

2 Open the **File** menu and select **Print…**

3 If you want to change the **Printer**, select one from the drop-
down list.

4 Set the **Print Range**. This can be *All* pages, the *Current Page*, the *Selection* only, or identified *Pages* – give single page numbers or page ranges separated by commas, e.g. 1,4,7 or 2-5,8.

5 Set the **Number of copies**. If **Collate** is off, multiple copies of each page will be printed in turn; if **Collate** is on, all the pages for the first copy will be printed before starting the next.

6 Click **OK** to print.

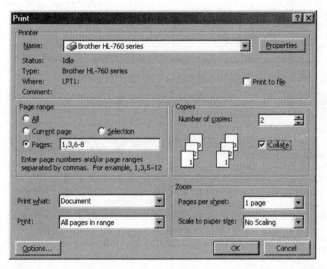

Figure 2.14 The **Print** dialog box – open this if you need to change any of the settings before printing.

Print preview

Word is a WYSIWYG (What You See Is What You Get) system, so that – as long as you work in Page Layout view – you can tell fairly accurately how your document will appear when it is printed. For an even better idea, use **File > Print Preview** to switch to the Print Preview display. This shows the pages exactly as they will be when printed, and has a Zoom facility that allows you to move in closer to check details easily.

2.9 Exercise

This exercise will provide practice in the skills and techniques in the word processing section of the CLAIT Level 1 syllabus.

Write a covering letter to accompany an application form for a job, along the lines of the one illustrated in Figure 2.15. The content is up to you, but the formatting should have these features:

- The font used throughout should be changed from the default Times New Roman to Georgia or Lucida Bright.
  Tip: set the font at the start.
- Your address should be centred, italic and 11 point.
- The rest of the letter should be set to 12 point.

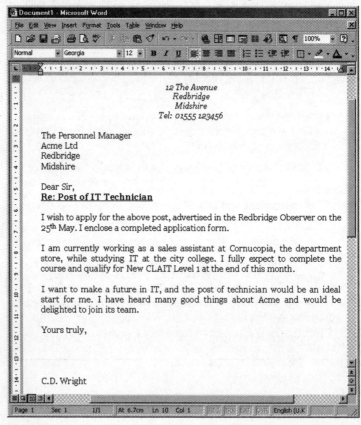

Figure 2.15 A sample letter.

Tip: set the size after formatting the address, but before typing the rest of the letter.

• The firm's address, greeting and reference should be left aligned.

• The reference line should underlined and bold.

• The main text of the letter should be justified. It should consist of at least three paragraphs, with blank lines between them.

When you have finished the letter, spell check it, then save it as 'Jobletter.doc' and print a copy.

Summary

• If you just want to type and edit plain text, a text editor will do the job; if you also want to format the text, you need a word processor.

• Microsoft Word is the world's leading word processor.

• Selected text can be copied, moved or deleted. You can select any amount of text, from a single character to the whole document.

• Use the Find routine to track down text in a long document, and Replace to change one word for another throughout a document.

• Text formatting allows you to set the font, size, colour, style and other aspects of the appearance of characters.

• The alignment, indents and spacing formatting options can only be applied to whole paragaphs.

• Use the spell checker to spot spelling and typing errors.

• A document can be saved as a file on disk for future reuse.

• You can print quickly with the current settings by clicking the toolbar Print button.

• For controlled printing, work through the Print dialog box.

03 electronic communication

In this chapter you will learn

- about e-mail and Outlook Express
- how to read and send messages
- how to send files by e-mail
- about the internet and IE
- how to browse and search the web

3.1 What is e-mail?

Electronic communication has dramatically changed the way that we do business and keep in touch with friends and family. Fast, efficient and cheap, e-mail is now one of the most used means of communication, particularly between international contacts, while the World Wide Web has given us easy access to huge stores of information and a vast array of services.

Electronic mail is the simplest and the most widely used of all the Internet facilities – in fact, some people find that e-mail is virtually their only use of the Internet. It is directly equivalent to ordinary 'snail' mail, except that messages are written on screen and sent via the Internet. To be able to send and receive e-mail, you need an e-mail account, which is normally allocated to you when you sign on with an Internet service provider or when you join a place of work or study.

E-mail is mainly used for sending plain text messages, but you can attach graphics, sounds, word-processed documents and other document files to e-mail messages.

E-mail is a fast and very efficient way to communicate. Even a long text message will be only a few kilobytes and can be sent off in a minute or two. Delivery is not quite instantaneous – messages will sometimes get through in seconds, but a few minutes is more typical. Of course, when they get read is another matter. Some of us only pick up our mail once a day, and don't always read all of the messages when they arrive.

E-mail can be written and read while you are online, but is best managed *offline*. This way, you are only online to your service for as long as it takes to transmit pre-written messages and to download incoming mail, saving this to disk. It doesn't just reduce your costs, it also avoids the possibility of losing a connection half-way through writing a message, and it gives you time to check your text for typing and spelling errors first.

When sending messages, you must get the e-mail addresses exactly right, or the post won't get through. There are tools and Web directories to help you find addresses, but the simplest way is to ring up your contacts and ask them to send you an e-mail. Their address will be visible in their mail.

3.2 E-mail addresses

Before you can write to anyone, you must know their address. Addresses follow simple rules and are fairly easy to remember, but you cannot work them out for yourself and you must get them exactly right. The pattern is:

> name@site.address

Notice the punctuation – an @ sign after the name, and dots between the constituent parts of the site address.

The **name** is usually based on the user's real name, though how it is formed depends on the organization. 'Johnny B. Goode', for example, might be allocated the names 'jbgoode', 'John_Goode', 'johnny.b.goode', 'johnnybg', 'goode123' or other variations. Underline (_) and dot (.) are often used to separate words, and a number may be added. Some organizations ignore the real name and allocate numbers or special user names.

The **site address** is often the same as that of the organization to which the user belongs, though some service providers allocate a separate domain name to each of their members.

The following examples are of names that have been allocated to me while I have been trying out different service providers:

> macbride@tcp.co.uk
>
> macbride@macdesign2000.freeserve.co.uk
>
> mac_bride@hotmail.com

Finding addresses

The simplest way to get someone's address is to ask them to send you an e-mail. When the message comes in it will have their address at the top, and you can be confident that it is exactly right.

You can only ask people for e-mail if you can contact them already, by phone or post. If not, there are several 'people-finding' directories on the Web – and it is often worth trying more than one. No directory holds the names of everyone on the Internet. Each has its own database, built by drawing on the members' lists of service providers, with more addresses that people have registered when visiting the directories.

Among the biggest people-finder sites are:

WhoWhere   www.whowhere.com
Bigfoot   www.bigfoot.com
InfoSpace   www.infospace.com
   or www.infospace.co.uk

You can reach these through your browser or through the *Find People* routine in Windows. The sites can all do approximate searches, to cope with variations in names. When looking for my old mate 'Clive Gladstone Postlethwaite', I don't know if he will be listed by this name or by his usual 'Clive Postlethwaite', or just by his initials and surname. A search for 'C Postlethwaite' should pick up all variations – and anyone else with the same surname and initial, but there shouldn't be too many of these. Tracking down your old mate 'John Smith' may not be as simple.

3.3 Outlook Express

Outlook Express is the e-mail software that accompanies Internet Explorer (see page 89) and is normally supplied with Windows. It is efficient and easy to use, though there are plenty of features for advanced users.

You will soon find your way around the screen display. The key components are:

◆ The list of folders for incoming, outgoing, recently deleted and saved mail.

   The *Inbox* is where new messages arrive, and that they will remain there until you delete them or move them to another folder; and the *Outbox* is where outgoing messages are stored if you write them when you are offline.

◆ The header pane is where you will see a list of the messages in the currently selected folder. It shows for each message the sender, subject and date (other details can also be displayed).

◆ The preview pane displays the text of the message selected in the header pane.

There are also a number of other elements, but – apart from the header pane – all are optional and can be easily switched off if you decide that you do not want them. I prefer a simple display.

Toolbar   Folder bar   Header pane

Outlook bar   Folder list   Views bar

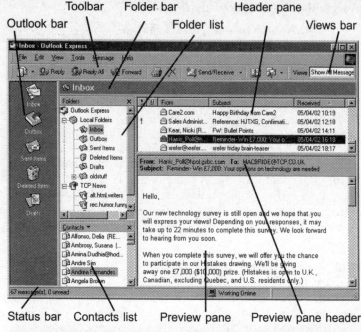

Status bar   Contacts list   Preview pane   Preview pane header

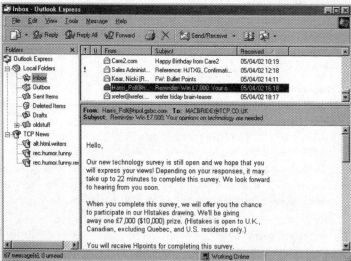

Figure 3.1 The Outlook Express screen has many elements, most of them optional – and best turned off! You can also turn off the Preview pane and read messages in a new window.

To control the layout:

1 Open the **View** menu and select **Layout...** to open this dialog box.

2 Tick the checkboxes to show, or clear them to hide the components.

3 If you want the Preview pane, tick **Show preview pane** then decide where you want it.

4 Click **OK**.

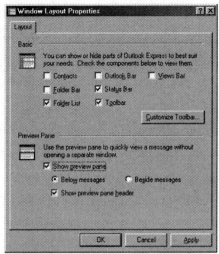

Figure 3.2 These settings produce the layout in the lower screenshot in Figure 3.1.

Setting the options

At some point, you should explore and adjust the options. The defaults work perfectly well, so don't rush into this and don't change a setting unless you are sure what to choose. The Send options are worth checking at an early stage.

To change the options:

1 Open the **Tools** menu and select **Options...**

2 At the **Options** dialog box, click the **Send** label to open its tab.

3 Set options as required, using these notes for guidance.

◆ **Save copy of sent messages in the 'Sent Items' folder** should be on only if you need a record of everything you send. To keep a copy of a single message, you can save it before you send it.

◆ **Send messages immediately** will start up the Connect routine (if you are not online) and send the message as soon as you have finished writing it. If you often write several messages at a time, turn this off, and use the **Send/Receive** button to send them all at once after you have finished writing.

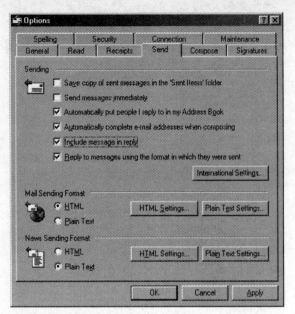

Figure 3.3 The Send options should be set early on.

- **Automatically put people I reply to in my Address Book** is worth turning on, as it ensures that you have their addresses.

- **Automatically complete e-mail addresses when composing** is worth having. When you are writing an e-mail, you can enter an address by picking it from the Address Book or by typing it. With this on, you may only need to type two or three letters.

- **Include messages in reply** is best turned off, for home users. Business users may prefer to have a copy of the original message in the reply, so that it can be answered point by point.

- **Reply to messages using the format in which they were sent** will ensure that your replies are in Plain Text or HTML to match the format of the incoming messages – so that you won't be sending HTML to people who can only handle Plain Text.

4 Click [OK] to save your settings and close the box.

3.4 The Address Book

E-mail addresses are a pain to type. They are rarely easy to remember and if you get just one letter wrong, the message won't
get through. The solution is to use the Address Book that is supplied with Outlook Express. Once an address is in here it can be
recalled by picking it from the list, or by typing the first few letters of the name.

To add an address to your Address Book:

1 Open the **Tools** menu and select **Address Book...** or click the
   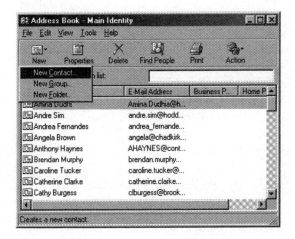 button.

2 When the Address Book opens, click the **New** button and select **New Contact...**

3 Type in the person's name, splitting it into **First, Middle** and
   Last – the separate parts can be used for sorting the list. You
   can miss out any you don't need, or even put the whole name
   into one slot.

4 Type the address in the **E-mail addresses** slot, then click
   Add .

5 Switch to the **Home** or **Business** tab if you want to store the
   snail mail address or phone number.

6 Click OK .

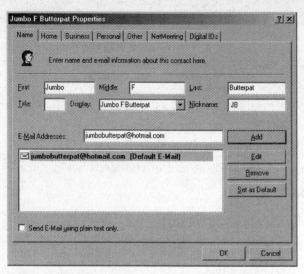

Figure 3.4 Creating a new entry in the Address Book in Outlook Express. Double-check that the address is exactly right!

3.5 Sending messages

You start with a *File – New message* command or click the **New Message** button to open the mail composition window. The main part of this is the editor, but in the top part of the window there are several boxes which must be attended to.

You will find three boxes, headed **To:**, **CC:** and **Subject:**.

* **To:** as you would expect, is the address of the recipient.
* **Cc:** is for the addresses of those to whom you want to send copies.

  You may also have a **Bcc:** (Blind carbon copy) box. These are not listed, as To and Cc recipients are, at the top of the message.

* **Subject:** should have a few words outlining the nature of your message. This will let your recipients know what's coming and help them to organize their mail folders.

Outlook Express, like most modern mail software, offers the sort of capabilities that you would find in a word processor. There are the normal range of fonts, size, style, colour and alignment options. You can write hyperlinks in your messages, so that your readers can go straight to a page – as long as their mail software

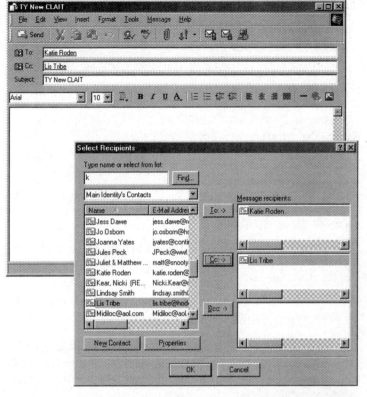

Figure 3.5 Starting to send a message. The first stage is to type the addresses or select them from the Address Book. Note that the message's Subject appears in the Title bar of the window.

can handle the link! You can also insert images, or text from other documents.

You do not have to format your messages. If you prefer – or if your recipients can't handle the formatting – you can send messages in plain text. This is perfectly adequate for most purposes and the files are a little smaller, and so are transferred a little faster.

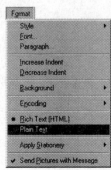

To switch between formatted – Rich Text (HTML) – and plain text messages, use the options on the **Format** menu in the **New Message** window.

To create a new message:

1. Use **File > New > Mail Message** or click [image].
2. Click [image] to open the Address Book (see page 77).
3. Select the recipient and click **To: ->** or **Cc: ->** to add the address to the **To** or **Cc** sets.
4. Click **OK**.
5. Type a **Subject** – keep it brief but clear.
6. Type your message.
7. Click **Send**. The message will either be sent immediately or placed in your Outbox for mailing when you next click **Send/Receive**.

Check your spelling!

Even though e-mail is generally treated as a casual form of communication, spell-checking is still worthwhile – some mistypes can be causes of great confusion!

- Click [image] to start the spell checker – it is used in exactly the same way as in Word (see page 62).

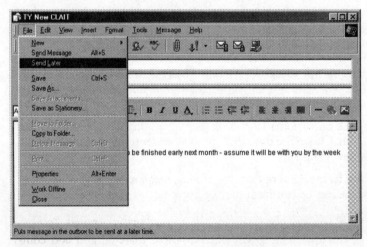

Figure 3.6 Messages can be sent immediately or stored in the Outbox for later delivery.

Stationery

Outlook Express offers 'stationery' for your messages, with a decorative background and the fonts ready-formatted.

To use stationery, click the drop-down arrow by the New Mail button and choose a style, then complete the message and send as normal.

3.6 Incoming mail

It may be obvious, but it is worth stating that e-mail does not get delivered directly to you. Instead, it goes into a mailbox at your service provider and you must log in to get it. (This is not true if you are on a network in an organization, where the network management software will collect mail for everyone and distribute it.)

Some services will automatically delete your mail from the mailbox once you have collected a copy; others will give you the option of leaving it there or deleting it. Opt to have it deleted. There is little point in keeping it, and they may charge you for storage beyond a certain point.

New mail is placed in the Inbox, where it will appear as a single line entry showing the sender, the date and whatever the sender wrote in their Subject line. After looking at the sender and the subject, you can decide whether you want to read it immediately, later or not at all. (There is a certain amount of junk mail that can find its way into your box.) If you store messages for long-term reference, the Subjects will help to identify them.

Click on a header to read its message in the Preview pane, if it is open. Otherwise double-click on a header to open the message in a new window.

You have several options for dealing with incoming mail. Most of these can be run from toolbar buttons.

- **Reply**, including the original text, if desired. You can edit that text, to cut out unwanted material and add comments.

- **Reply to all** – if you are one of several people receiving a copy of the message – you can send the reply to them all.

*   ![Forward icon] **Forward** the mail to someone else, perhaps after editing.
*   **Save** the message as a plain text file.
*   ![Print icon] **Print** the message.
*   **Copy or cut** part of the message, pasting it into a word processed file, using the standard Windows Edit routines.
*   ![Delete icon] **Delete** the message.
*   **Move** the message to another folder, by dragging it from the message list into the target folder.

Replying or forwarding will open the New Message window, and copy in the sender's address and the message.

3.7   Files by mail

Binary files (images, programs, documents and other data) can be sent by mail, attached to messages. As the mail system was designed for transmitting plain text, binary files must be converted to text for transfer, and back to binary on receipt. This is a technical and sometimes quite tricky operation if you have to do it yourself. Fortunately, Outlook Express comes with built-in routines to handle these conversions. All you have to do is identify the file to attach, or select a folder in which to store an incoming attachment.

I use attachments regularly to send Word documents, samples, images – even whole books – to people, and it is generally very reliable, but there are a few snags you should be aware of. Most of these revolve around the size of binary files, which tend to be large – especially compared to simple text messages.

When a file is converted for transmission, it gets about 50% bigger, and it can take a while to send – or receive – messages with attachments. For example, the screenshot opposite is just under 700Kb, and as an attached file would be a little over 1Mb. E-mail is transmitted at around 3Kb per second, so it would take around 5 minutes to send this picture.

If an e-mail transfer is interrupted part-way through – because of a faulty line, overcrowding at the service provider or whatever – it has to start again from scratch. Interruptions are more likely with larger files, simply because you have to be online longer.

When you pick up your mail, it is downloaded from your service provider in the order that it was received, and if there is a huge attachment to an early message, you will have to get that before you can pick up later ones. This can be a real pain, especially if you know that there is an urgent message somewhere down the line. Be kind! Don't send people big binaries unless they really want them!

And finally, do note that not everyone has e-mail software that can handle attachments – if yours can't, upgrade now – so check that your recipients can cope before relying on attachments for anything vital.

To attach a file:

1 Start to create a new message as usual.
2 Open the **Insert** menu and select **File Attachment…** or click 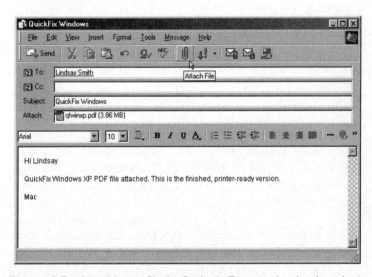.
3 Locate and select the file and click **Attach**.
4 Repeat for other files, if wanted.
5 Complete and send the message.

Figure 3.7 Attaching a file in Outlook Express is simple – just click the button and locate the file.

Detaching files

Detaching files is simple. Files can be opened directly from the message, or saved to disk for viewing later. *Caution is essential as computer viruses can be spread through attached files.*

1 Select the message.

2 Click ✐ in the Preview pane header.

3 If you want to save the file(s), click **Save Attachments...**

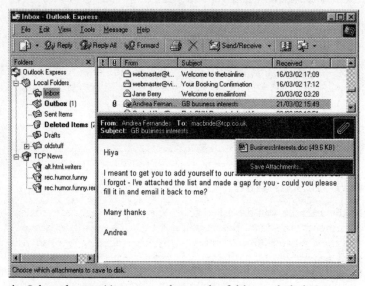

4 Select the one(s) to save, choose the folder and click **Save**.

5 To open a file, select it from the list.

6 At the **Warning** prompt, select **Open it** if you are sure it is safe, and click **OK**. The file will be opened if your PC has a program that can handle it. You may be asked which program to use to open it with.

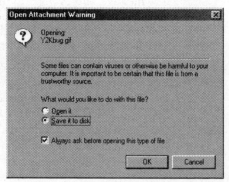

Avoiding viruses

Follow these rules to reduce the chances of your computer being infected by viruses:

◆ *Never* open a file from an unknown source.

◆ Only open files from known sources if you are expecting them – some viruses send themselves out as e-mails under other people's names.

◆ Never open an executable file – one with a .exe, .com, .bat, .vb extension – unless you are quite certain what it will do.

◆ Word documents may have viruses hidden in macros. Make sure that the Security level in Word is set to high – use **Tools > Macro > Security** to set the level.

◆ Install anti-virus software and use it.

3.8 Exercise: Using e-mail

In this exercise you are asked to arrange a meeting and circulate documents via e-mail. Before you start, get the e-mail addresses – and the cooperation! – of at least two other people. You will also need a short Word document. This might be the proposed agenda for the meeting.

1 Decide which file to attach, or create a new one, and make sure that you know where it is stored.

2 Start a new message, addressing it to the people who you want to be at the meeting. They should all be in the **To** box. If there are people that you want to inform about the meeting – but their presence is not expected – send them **Cc** copies.

3 Give the message a clear Subject line and add a brief covering message.

4 Attach the document – you do know where it is, don't you?

5 Send the message.

When the message reaches its recipients, here's what they need to do:

6 Open the message, then open the attached file.

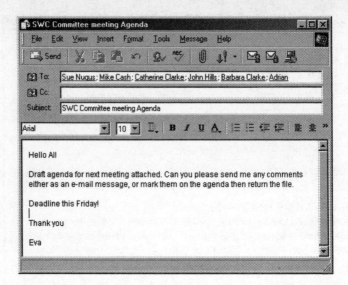

7   To return the document, with corrections, additions or anno-
    tations, open the **File** menu, point to **Send To** and select **Mail
    Recipient (As Attachment)**. This will start up the New Mes-
    sage window, with the document already attached. The mes-
    sage can then be completed and sent as normal.

3.9   The Internet

First of all, the Internet is *not* the World Wide Web. The Internet
is the hardware – the computers and the connections between
them – and the software that let them communicate with each
other. Over 30 million computers (and more every day) are permanently connected to the Internet and offer services to its users.
Some of these *hosts* store information – text, pictures, sound or
video files; some provide interactive services to visitors; some are
connections in the network, collecting and passing on messages
between computers; some are servers at Internet service providers,
allowing ordinary users – you and me – to connect to the Internet
and to store our own Web pages. And when you go online, your
computer becomes part of the Internet.

The host computers are run by government agencies, firms, universities, and other bodies. The connections between them are a
mixture of public and private telephone lines, cables and micro-
wave links. No single organization owns or controls the Internet –

the nearest thing you have to central control are the agencies which allocate names to Web sites (to avoid duplication). It may sound chaotic, but it works!

The Internet grew out of a 1960s US Government project to develop a communications system that would survive a nuclear attack. Fortunately, it has never been needed for that, and just as fortunately it was allowed to expand. It spread first into military and research establishments within the USA and overseas, linking the networks in each organization into an *internetwork*. Some US universities set up their own internetwork links, and these linked into the Government's net in the mid-1980s to form the core of the Internet. Since then, it has expanded enormously, so that now most of the world's universities, many of its schools, most businesses large and small, most governments and political parties, pressure groups and charities, are online.

It is an important point that the Internet was not set up as a commercial venture. Even today, when many businesses are advertising and selling goods and services on the Internet, a large part of it remains non-commercial. Much of the data that flows across the Net is generated by people having fun – sharing ideas and tracking down information on their enthusiasms, keeping in touch with remote friends, old and new, playing games, or just plain 'surfing' to see what they can find.

Many millions of people now have access to the Internet, either through their work/school/college or from home. At the time of writing, the best estimates are that around 20 million people in the UK are online – that's about a third of the population. The proportion is similar in the USA, in Europe and the rest of the developed world, and lower – but growing fast – elsewhere.

The World Wide Web

This is the most colourful, exciting and, for many users, the most useful aspect of the Internet. It consists of billions of *pages* of information, stored on host computers throughout the world. The pages contain text, graphics, video clips, sounds and – most importantly – *hyperlinks*. A hyperlink can be attached to a text item or image and will connect it to another page, which may be in the same computer, or in another machine the other side of the World. Hyperlinks can also be used to connect to files, e-mail addresses and other Internet resources.

How hyperlinks work

When the HTML document is written, to create the Web page, a hyperlinked phrase or image has attached to it the URL – the Internet address – of another page or file. Clicking on the phrase or image makes the Web browser pick up this URL and send it down the line to the remote computer. This makes the connection to whichever server hosts the linked page, and passes the connection back to you. The links are processed and documents transferred using HTTP, the HyperText Transfer Protocol. This is why the URLs of Web pages start with '**http://**'.

To access the World Wide Web, you need a *web browser* – a program that can display the text and images that make up Web pages and interpret the hyperlinks that will take you from one page to another. With the aid of and plug-ins and linked applications, browsers can also handle all kinds of graphics formats, audio/video clips, multimedia displays, virtual reality and other types of files that are sometimes found on the Web. The Web browser most commonly used today is Internet Explorer.

The Web is an open system – anyone can publish their material there. Individuals and organizations run sites for many reasons: as a public service, as an academic exercise or resource for students, or simply as a means of sharing their interests with others. Some Web pages are excellent sources of information in their own right, some are treasure troves of links to other valuable pages; and some are pure trivia. All large businesses and many smaller ones now have Web sites to advertise and perhaps sell their products. For some firms, the site *is* the business. They provide information and services to encourage people to spend time there – and to see the advertisements that provide the income.

Despite the massive quantity of information that is on the Web, finding the things that interest you is not usually that difficult.

* *Directories* have organized links to selected Web sites and pages. Yahoo! is probably the best known of these, and is an excellent place at which to start researching a subject.
* At *search engines* you can hunt for pages that contain given words. They are most useful when you are looking for infor-

mation on a specific topic as they can pick out relevant pages from the billions on the Web. You have to define your search accurately with some of these, or you may be swamped by the thousands of links that they will find for you!

Uniform Resource Locators (URL)

Every page on the Web – and, in fact, every file of any kind on the Internet – can be identified by a URL. There are different styles of URL for each approach to the Internet, though they all follow much the same pattern:

type://hostcomputer/directory/filename

Web pages can usually be recognized by their *html* or *htm* endings, which shows that they are hypertext pages.

http://sunsite.unc.edu/boutell/faq/www-faq.html

This one is a list of frequently asked questions (*faq*) and their answers, about the World Wide Web (*www*), stored in the Sun archives (*sunsite*) at the University of North California (*unc.edu*).

http://homepages.tcp.co.uk/~macbride

Here's my home page, in case you want to drop by. Like the URLs of many personal home pages, this consists of the address of a computer at my service provider, followed by a tilde (~) and my user name.

The URL of the top page of a site may just consist of the site address, with an (optional) slash at the end:

http://www.microsoft.com/

This will take you to the opening page at Microsoft's site.

3.10 Internet Explorer

Internet Explorer is distributed as part of the Windows package and as a component in the Office suites. The examples and screenshots in this chapter are mainly from IE5, but the earlier IE 4.0 and the current IE 6.0 (supplied with Windows XP) are little different.

The Explorer screen

Around the main page display area there are a number of control bars, almost all of which can be turned on or off. (If your screen display is 800×640 or less, or you run your browser at less than full size, you may find it difficult to read Web pages with all the control bars open.)

+ The Explorer bar can be opened to display the History (pages visited recently), Favorites or an online Search.

+ The Menu bar gives you access to all commands, but the most-used ones can also be reached through the Toolbar.

Menu bar   Address bar   Toolbar

Explorer bar   Radio   Links

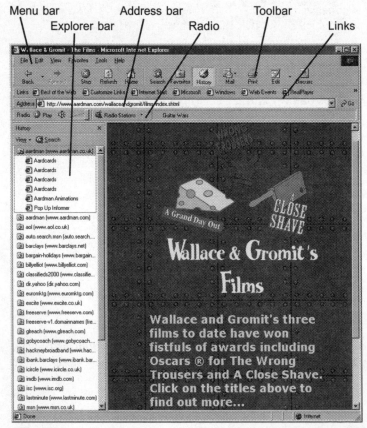

Figure 3.8 The IE screen, with the Explorer bar displaying the History.

- The **Address** bar shows the address of the page. You can type a URL here to go to a page.
- The **Links** bar contains ready-made links to some useful sites. Just click on the link to go to its page.
- The **Radio** bar lets you link to an Internet radio broadcast for music (or news, sports reports or whatever) while you surf. (In IE 6.0, the Radio bar is replaced by the Media option in the Explorer bar. It still links to Internet radio stations, but also gives access to other online media facilities.)

The Toolbar buttons

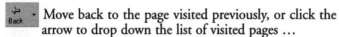 Move back to the page visited previously, or click the arrow to drop down the list of visited pages …

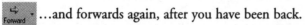 …and forwards again, after you have been back.

Stop downloading the current page.

Reload the page – use this if a page fails to load properly.

Go to your home page.

Run an online Search in Explorer bar.

Open the Favorites list in Explorer bar (page 93).

Open the History list in Explorer bar (page 92).

Run your e-mail software to read mail or send a message.

Print the current page.

Edit the page (if it has been saved on your hard disk).

3.11 Browsing the Web

Once you have got to a good starting point in the Web, you can usually surf a long way by following up hyperlinks. But how do you get to that starting point?

At first, you have three main options:

* Click **Home** to go to the default home page at MSN – Microsoft Network – or your service provider. You should find some useful starting points there.
* Click one of the **Links** buttons. These lead to different starting points within MSN.
* Use the **Address** box – type in the URL of the page and press [**Enter**]. Typed addresses are stored, like the History, and can be reused by selecting them from the drop-down list.

After you have been using Explorer for a while, there are two other approaches that you can use.

History

As you browse, the places that you visit are stored in the History, and you can revisit these by opening History in the Explorer bar and selecting them from there.

Pages are normally grouped into site folders, within date folders. To reach a page, open the folder for the date, then the folder for the site and click on the page name.

If the name is in black, the page can be displayed offline. If it is in grey, either IE has dumped the files to save space, or the page has active content which can only be seen online.

The default setting is for the History list to be organized **By Date**, but using the **View** options, you can instead list the pages **By Site**, **Most Visited** or **Order Visited Today**.

* Use **Order Visited Today** instead of the Back button's drop-down list to return to a page visited early on in the current session. The History is far more reliable that the Back button, which often loses track of where it has been!

Set the list order   Click to open/close History

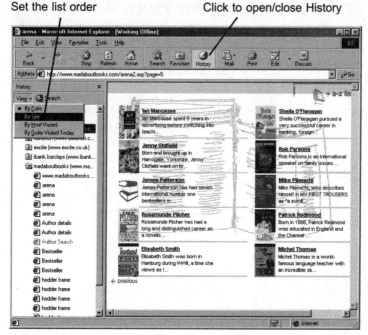

Figure 3.9 Using the History to revisit sites.

Favorites

The History records your visits, but keeps links for a limited time. If you want a permanent link to a page, add it to your *Favorites*.

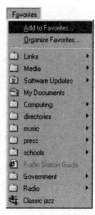

*   When you are at a site that you know you want to revisit, click **Favorites** and select **Add to Favorites**.

*   When you want to return to the page, either click ![Favorites] to display your Favorites in the Explorer bar, or open the **Favorites** menu. Click on a link, opening folders as needed.

When your Favorites list gets so long that you can't find things quickly, it's time to organize it by moving related items into suitable folders.

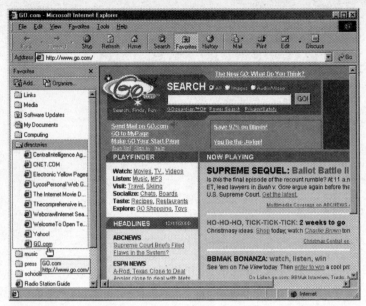

Figure 3.10 Picking up a link from the Favorites. When you point to a link, a pop-up shows its full name – if this is not already visible.

1 Click **Organize Favorites** on the **Favorites** menu or in the Explorer bar.

2 Click **Create Folder** and give the new folder a name.

Click on a folder to open it, if you want to move a link out of a folder.

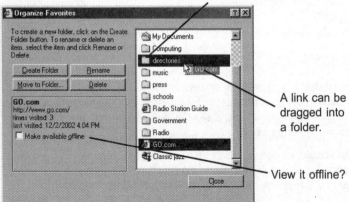

A link can be dragged into a folder.

View it offline?

Figure 3.11 Try to keep your Favorites organized.

3   To move a link into a folder, simply drag it over to the folder and drop it in.

Or

◆   Select the link and click **Move to Folder**, then select the folder from the list.

Offline viewing

It often takes less time to download a page – especially if it is mainly text – than it does to read it. If there are sites that you want to read regularly, you can get IE to download their top pages – and the ones linked to them – in one continuous operation. You can then read the pages offline, reconnecting if there are links that you want to follow up. To set up a Favorite for this, tick the **Make available offline** box, and click the **Properties** button to set the options. IE5 will download the top page and as many levels of linked pages as you want, and do it automatically or when you use the **Tools > Synchronize** command.

3.12   Search engines

If you want to find some specific information on the Web, the best place to start is a *search engine*. This is a site which has software that constantly scans the Web, building an indexed database of pages, which it allows visitors to search. Search engines vary in the way they collect and hold data, and in their degree of completeness – a 100% coverage is impossible as pages are being added and changed constantly. If you don't find what you want at one, it is often worth trying another.

At present, Google is the best search engine. It has a massive database – over 2 billion Web pages – but is extremely fast and it has a very clever ranking system which normally brings the best pages to the top of the results list. (The 'best' pages are those that match your search most closely, and which have most visitors and most links from other sites.)

You should always try to be as specific as you can. For example, a search for 'football' found 14.3 million pages, and the top ones were all American football. The more closely specified search for 'football world cup tickets' produced around 7,000 hits, and the FIFA world cup site was right at the top.

Searching at Google is simple:

1 Go to **www.google.com**
2 Type in one or more words to describe what you are looking for.
3 Click **Google Search**.
4 Scan through the results and click on a link to go to its page.

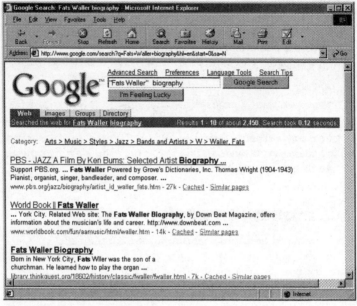

Figure 3.12 The results of a search at Google – and I found all that I needed about Fats Waller in the first few linked pages.

AltaVista is another fast and powerful search engine. It allows you to ask your questions in plain English – although it only actually looks at key words in a question. For example, 'steam railways in Wales' will produce the same results as 'Where can I find out about steam railways in Wales' – and take half as long to type!

Some features of AltaVista are well worth noting.

◆ You can also search for images, video and audio clips.

◆ The results are accompanied by some suggestions for questions which may help you find what you want.

◆ It doesn't just handle plain *English*, you can run a search in any major language.

3.13 Data from Web pages

Saving pages

There are four main ways to save information from Web pages. You can save a page, with or without its embedded images, sounds and other files; you can save a single image from a page; or a selected chunk of text.

To save a page:

1 Open the **File** menu and select **Save As…**
2 Go to the required folder.
3 Edit the **File name** to identify the page clearly.
4 If you just want a page's text, set the **Save as type** to *Text file*.
5 To save the page complete with its images and other files set the **Save as type** to *Web Page complete*. The files will be saved in a folder with a related name. E.g. if the page is 'Mt Etna.htm', the files will be stored in 'Mt Etna_files'.
6 Click **Save**.

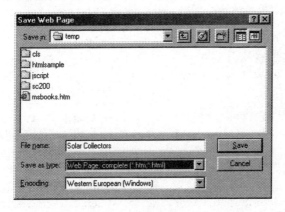

You can now view the page offline and whenever you like, by opening the page's file on your hard disk.

To save an image:

◆ Right-click on the image and select **Save Picture As…**, then complete the **Save As** dialog box as normal.

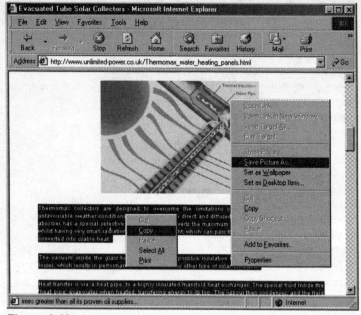

Figure 3.13 Images or blocks of text can be saved or copied.

To save selected text:

• Highlight the text, then right-click on it and select **Copy**. Paste it into Word and save it from there.

Printing Web pages

The current Web page can be printed, once it has fully loaded. As Web pages are designed for the screen, they may not fit comfortably onto A4 sheets of paper.

To print the entire page:

• Click the **Print** button ![Print icon] – that's it!

To print part of the page:

1 Select the text and images that you want to print.
2 Open the **File** menu and select **Print…**
3 In the **Print** range, click **Selection**.
4 Click **OK**.

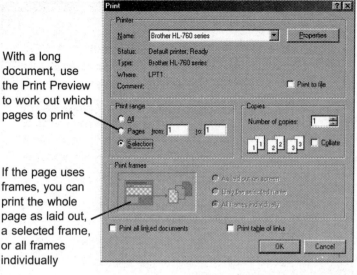

With a long document, use the Print Preview to work out which pages to print

If the page uses frames, you can print the whole page as laid out, a selected frame, or all frames individually

Figure 3.14 Work through the Print dialog box if you want anything more than a single copy of the whole of the current page, and if it is much more than a screenful, preview it first to see how it will fit on the pages.

3.14 Exercise: Searching the Web

1 Go to Google (www.google.com) and run a search for a historical character of your choice.

2 Follow up some of the resulting links, aiming to locate at least three pages containing relevant material.

3 Save one page complete with all its files.

4 From a second page, copy the headline and the first few paragraphs of text, and paste it into a new Word document. Save the file.

5 Save an image from another page.

Summary

◆ E-mail is a very efficient form of communication.

◆ Outlook Express is the e-mail software supplied with Internet Explorer. Set its options to suit the way you work.

◆ You must know people's e-mail address before you can write to them. You may be able to find a person's address in one of the Internet's directories, but the best way to get it is to ask them to send you mail.

◆ Addresses can be stored in the Address Book.

◆ When sending mail, you should include a Subject line so that your recipients know what's coming.

◆ After reading an incoming message, you can reply to it, forward it on to someone else, delete it or move or copy it for long-term storage.

◆ Files can be sent by mail, attached to messages.

◆ Internet Explorer is the world's leading browser. It is simple to use, but powerful and fully-featured.

◆ Once you have got started on the Web, you can browse by following hyperlinks.

◆ Links to pages can be stored in the Favorites so that they are at hand next time you want to visit.

◆ The History keeps a record of visited sites, making it simple to go back to a page.

◆ If it's anywhere on the Internet, a good search engine such as Google, can find it for you.

◆ You can save complete Web pages, or selected text or images.

04

spreadsheets

In this chapter you will learn

- what a spreadsheet is
- how to enter and edit data
- how to write formulae and use functions
- how to format text and numbers
- how to insert and delete rows and columns
- how to print a spreadsheet

4.1 What is a spreadsheet?

Excel is a spreadsheet application. A spreadsheet (also called a *worksheet*) consists of a grid of cells into which text, numbers and formulae can be written. An Excel sheet has 256 columns and 65,536 rows – that's over 16 million cells! And you can link any number of sheets together in a *workbook*. In addition to the basic storing and calculating facilities, Excel offers:

* ready-made functions and wizards for perfoming complex calculations and data analysis;
* database-style sorting and searching;
* full control over the layout and appearance;
* easy-to-use routines for turning figures into graphs that can make underlying trends and patterns more visible.

Spreadsheets have two layers

With a word-processed document, what you see is what you get. Spreadsheets are different. The data that you enter the sheet is not necessarily what you see on the screen or printed output. You (normally) see the the *results* of calculations, not the formulae; numbers can be shown in different formats (see page 110); the display of text may be cropped short if it is too long to fit into its cell; and confidential data can be hidden if desired. (Hiding data is not covered in the CLAIT syllabus.)

Cell references

Cell references are used in formulae to tell Excel where to find the values to work on.

* To identify a single cell, give the column letter followed by the row number, e.g. in the sheet shown below, the total is in E11.
* To identify a range of cells, give the references of the top left and bottom right cells, separated by a colon, e.g. the *Costs* in the example below are in the range E5:E9.
* A range can be a single line of cells in a row or column, or a block covering several rows and columns.

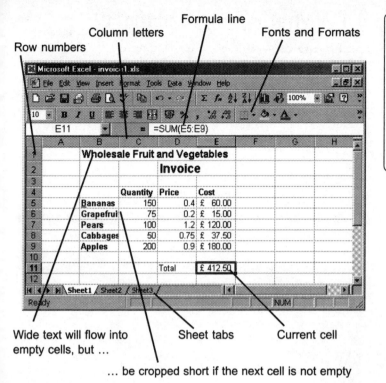

Row numbers

Column letters

Formula line

Fonts and Formats

Wide text will flow into empty cells, but …

Sheet tabs

Current cell

… be cropped short if the next cell is not empty

Figure 4.1 The Excel screen

4.2 Entering data

In Excel there are two distinct types of data: text and numbers. When entering data, you do not normally need to tell Excel which type it is – Excel can recognize the difference:

Fred Smith   is text

1 High Street is text (even though it starts with a digit

123   is a number

But watch out with telephone numbers – which should be treated as text, not number values.

    02075551234

would be treated as the number 2,075,551,234.

Write telephone numbers (and similar references or codes), either with spaces between their sections, or preceded by an apostrophe:

> 0207 555 1234

or   '02075551234

Data can be entered into any cell on the sheet, so you can lay out your text and figures just where you want them.

1 Click into the target cell.

To enter data:

2 Start to type. Notice that the typing appears both in the cell and in the Formula line.

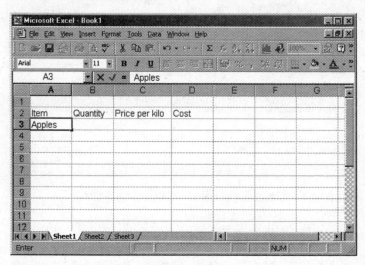

To edit data:

The cell's contents will be displayed in the Formula line.

3 Click into the Formula line, or press [**F2**] to start editing.

- Use the [←] / [→] keys to move the cursor.
- Press [**Backspace**] or [**Delete**] to erase errors.
- Type in new data as needed.

4 Click ☑ beside the Formula line, or press [**Enter**] when you have done.

4.3 Using formulae

Simple formulae are easy to create in Excel. If you want the total of a column or row, you can get it with a click of the **Autosum** button. Other calculations take a bit more effort, but point and click references, and ready-made functions simplify the process.

A formula starts with the = sign and can contain a mixture of cell references, numbers, text and functions, joined by operators.

Examples of simple formulae:

= 4 * C1   4 times the contents of cell C1

= B3+B4   the value in B3 added to that in B4

=SUM(A5:A12)   the sum of cells A5 to A12.

References can be typed into the Formula line, or pulled in by selecting the cells.

1   Click on the cell where the formula is to go.
2   Type '='.
3   Type the number, or point and click to get a cell reference.
4   Type an operator.

When Excel expects a reference, clicking on a cell writes the reference into the formula

Autosum

Figure 4.2   This formula (=B3*C3) will multiply the contents of B3 and C3. With the values shown here, it will display 250

5 Type the next number, or select the next reference.

6 Repeat steps 4 and 5, as necessary.

7 Press [**Enter**].

Arithmetic operators

These operators can be used to calculate values:

+ Addition

– Subtraction

* Multiplication

/ Division

( ) brackets

Excel follows the normal rules of arithmetic in its calculations. Where there are several operators in a formula, multiplication and division are calculated first, then addition and subtraction. If an operation is in brackets, it gets priority. e.g.

$$4 * 3 + 2 = 14$$

but $\quad 4 * (3 + 2) = 20.$

Copying formulae

Spreadsheets are normally used not for single calculations, but for processing larger quantities of data, and this often means that many of the formulae are very similar. For example, if a spreadsheet was being used to create an invoice, it would need to multiply the quantity and price for every item to find the cost for that line.

In the simple example shown here, D3 contains the formula:

=B3*C3

We want the same kind of Quantity * Price formula in the other Cost cells. We could go to each in turn and write a suitable formula, e.g.

in D4 =B4*C4

in D5 =B5*C5

But there is a better way.

Excel can copy formulae intelligently. If you copy the formula in D3 (=B3*C3) into D4, it will automatically adjust the row in the cell references so that it reads:

=B4*C4

This works because Excel treats these cell references as *relative*. It understands the formula to mean:

take the value in the cell two places to the left and multiply it by the value in the one next left

Another result of this is that if you insert or delete rows or columns, so that the cells in the formula are in a different place, Excel will automatically alter the references to suit.

New copies of a formula can be created one at a time, or a whole set at once. Try it.

1 Type in items, quantities and prices along the lines shown here – use your own data if you like – but fitting into the same cells.

2 In D3, create the first Cost formula:

=B3*C3

3 Right-click on D3 and select **Copy**.

4 Highlight the cells from D4 down to D8.

5 Right-click and select **Paste**. The formula will be copied into each of the cells, with the row references adjusted to suit.

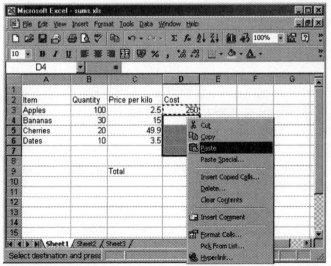

Figure 4.3 Formulae can be quickly copied with Cut and Paste.

4.4   Functions

A function is a predefined calculation. You give the function the cell references or values to work on, and it performs the calculation and displays the result.

All functions have the same shape: they consist of the function name, followed by brackets, in which the values or cell references are written.

Excel has a huge range of functions covering many different types of calculation. Some are quite complex – PMT() for example, calculates the mortgage repayments – others are much more straightforward.

Let's have a look at a simple function.

The Sum() function

Sum() calculates the total of the values in the referenced cells. It can be used to add up a set of individual values or cell references, e.g.

=SUM(2, 3, 4)   gives 9

=SUM(A1, A2, A3) adds the values in those cells

It is more commonly used to add up a column or row of figures, e.g.

=SUM(C2:C10)   adds the values in the cells from C2 to C10.

To write a formula using SUM():

1   Enter numbers into a short column of cells.

2   Click on the cell where you want the total – the one below the column is probably the best place.

3   Start to type the formula:

=SUM(

4   Point to the first cell in the set, hold down the left mouse button and drag a highlight over the others. The cell reference will appear in the formula.

5   Type the closing bracket ')'.

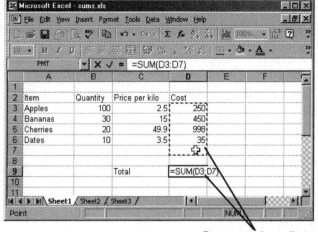

Drag over the cells to get the reference into the formula

4.5 Formatting

Text formatting

You can set the typeface, styles and sizes of text in almost exactly the same way as in Word. The biggest difference is that formatting can only be applied to whole cells, and not to selected text within a cell.

To format text:

1 Select the cell(s).

2 Click a toolbar button.

Or

3 Use **Format – Cells**, switch to the **Font** tab and use its wider range of format options.

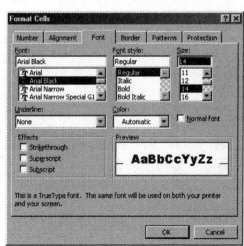

Number formatting

How we write a number depends on what it represents. If it is a money value, we would normally show two figures after the decimal point and add a currency sign (e.g. £); with a large number, we put a separator (usually a comma) every three digits to make it easier to read; if it is a percentage, we add % after it.

Excel can display numbers in several different formats including:

- **General** shows most values as *Number*, large ones as *Scientific*.
- **Number** is the natural format, with no punctuation and as many decimal places as were entered or were produced by a calculation.
- **Scientific** is a compact way to show very large or very small values, and need not worry us.
- **Comma** is a version of *Number*, with a separator every three digits, and showing two decimal places.

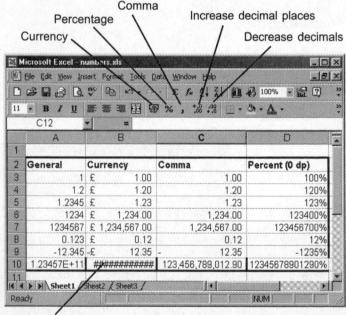

Figure 4.4 The format changes how a number appears, but does not affect its value – in this example, all the values in any one row are the same. If "#####" appears, it means that the column is not wide enough to display the number properly in that format.

- **Currency** as *Comma*, with a currency sign (e.g. £).
- **Percent** multiplies the value by 100 and adds % at the end.

Setting number formats

You can use the toolbar buttons to apply the Currency, Percentage or Comma styles, or to increase or decrease the number of decimal places. For any other settings, you need to go to the **Format Cells** dialog box.

1 Select the range of cells to be formatted.

2 From the **Format** menu select **Cells...**

3 On the **Number** tab, select a format from the **Category** list.

4 Set the number of decimal places.

5 With the *Number* and *Currency* formats, set the **Negative numbers** style.

6 With *Currency*, pick a **Symbol**.

7 Click **OK**.

The options vary to suit the Category.

As well as displaying numbers in different formats, Excel can also understand numbers written in different formats.

- Type in '£12,345.67' and it will realize that the underlying value is 12345.67 and that you want it displayed as currency.
- Type in 50% and it will store it as 0.5, while displaying 50%.
- Type in 0208-123 4567 and it will not be fooled into thinking it's a sum – this gets treated as text.

Try it and see for yourself.

Displayed and real values

Remember that what you see on screen is the *formatted* number – the real value is stored with 15-digit accuracy.

Alignment

By default, Excel aligns text to the left and numbers to the right. This normally works very well. Sometimes you will want to change the alignment, e.g. headings may look better centred, and when numbers are used as codes or references, they may be best aligned to the left, like text.

To change the alignment:

1 Select the cells.
2 Click the **Align Left**, **Center** or **Right** toolbar buttons.

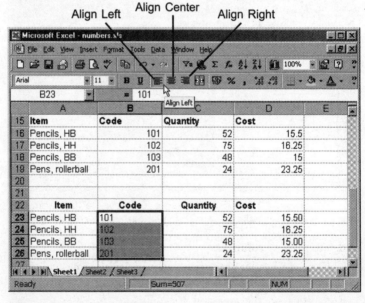

Figure 4.5 Changing the alignment. If you want numbers to align on the decimal stop, format them to display the same number of decimal places.

4.6 Rows and columns

The layout of a sheet can be adjusted at any stage. One of the most common kinds of amendment is adding or deleting rows and columns.

To add rows or columns:

1 Click on the row number or the column letter where you want to insert a new one.

2 If you want to insert more than one, drag across the letters or down the numbers for as many new rows or columns as you want.

3 Right-click on the highlighted area and select **Insert**.

The existing rows will be moved down (or columns to the right) to make way.

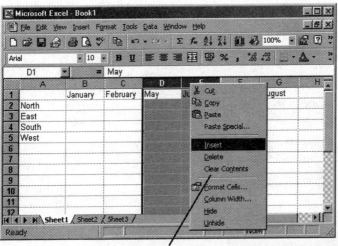

Use **Clear Contents** to delete the data from the cells without changing the shape of the sheet.

To delete rows or columns:

1 Click on the header of the first of the unwanted rows/columns and drag down or across to select any others.

2 Right-click on the area and select **Delete** from the shortcut menu.

The lines will be deleted and the gap closed.

Column width

If you want to fit a lot of columns of figures into one screen or page, you can reduce their width.

If the text or numbers in a cell cannot be displayed fully, you can make the column wider.

To adjust the column width:

1 Select the column(s) to be adjusted.

Either

2 Point to the dividing line between the header letters on the right-hand side of a column. The cursor will change to ✛

3 Drag the cursor to the left or right to increase/decrease the width. A dotted line will indicate the new column width.

4 Release the mouse button to set the width.

Or

5 Right-click on the columns and select **Column Width...** from the context menu.

6 Type in a new value – the width is measured in the number of digits (in 10 point font size) that will fit across the cell.

7 Click **OK**.

Drag the dividing line to set the width ...

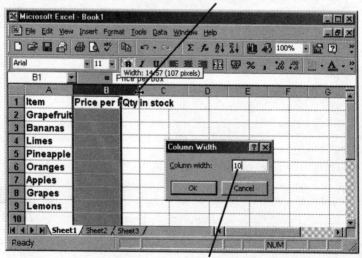

... or type in the new value

Row height

You are less likely to want to adjust this, as the row height changes automatically to suit the size of its contents. If you change the size of the font in any cell in a row, the height of the whole row will adjust to fit.

If you do want to change the height, you can do it as for column widths, dragging the ╪ cursor on the dividing line below the selected row.

If you use the **Row Height** option on the context menu, note that the height is set in points.

4.7 Documents and files

Files are opened, closed and saved in Excel in almost the same ways as in Word (see section 2.7).

Files are are normally saved in Microsoft Excel Workbook (.xls) format, though alternative formats are possible. For example, files could be saved in the CSV (Comma Separated Value) format for transfering data to a database.

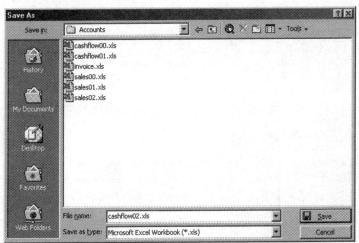

Figure 4.6 When saving worksheets – or any document – do make sure that the name identifies the file clearly!

Worksheets can be created from scratch, or based on a template. At some point, explore your system to see which templates are available as these ready-made solutions can save you a lot of time if there is one that meets your needs.

To start a new file:

1 Click the **New** button 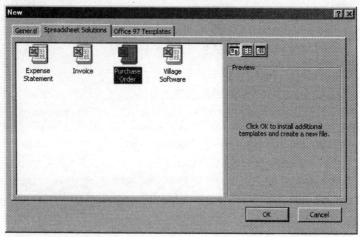 on the Standard toolbar to start from a blank worksheet.

Or

2 Open the **File** menu and select **New**, then select a template from one of the tabs on the New dialog box.

Figure 4.7 You may need the installation CD ROM to access some of the spreadsheet solutions.

4.8 Printing

Printing is not as straightforward in Excel as in some applications. A spreadsheets can be any size and use any layout, so the printout may fit on a single page or be spread across many. To get a good-looking printout you may have to adjust the orientation of the paper, the scale of the print and other aspects.

If the sheet will need more than one page, use the **Page Setup** panel to define how it will be split up for printing and to add headers/footers and other optional extras. Use the Print Preview to check that your setup works, before you commit it to paper.

Normally, the whole active area will be printed.

1 If you only want to print part of the sheet, select the cells, then use **File > Print area > Set print area** to define the print area.

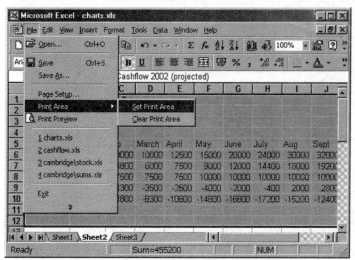

2 From the **File** menu select **Page Setup...**
3 On the **Page** tab, set the **Orientation** and **Scaling** – reduce large sheets or set the **Fit to** pages options.

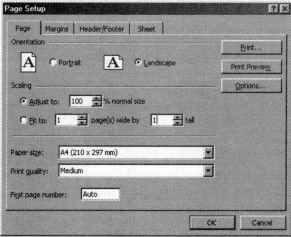

4 Click **Print Preview** and check the preview. If it needs adjusting, click **Setup...** to return to the Page Setup.

5 Click **Print…**
6 Set the **Print range**, **Number of copies** and other options as usual.
7 Click **OK**.

Displaying and printing formulae

Formulae are normally hidden, when they are not being written or edited in the Formula bar – which is good, because we are normally only interested in the results. Sometimes you need to be able to see and to print out the formulae in a sheet. Here's how.

To turn on the display of formulae:

1 Open the **Tools** menu and select **Options…**
2 In the **Options** dialog box, open the **View** tab.
3 In the **Window options** area, tick **Formulas**.
4 Click **OK**.

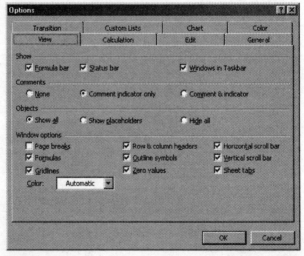

When you are returned to the sheet, you will find that the columns have all been widened to make room for the display of formulae.

To print formulae:

• Turn on the formula display then print the sheet as normal.

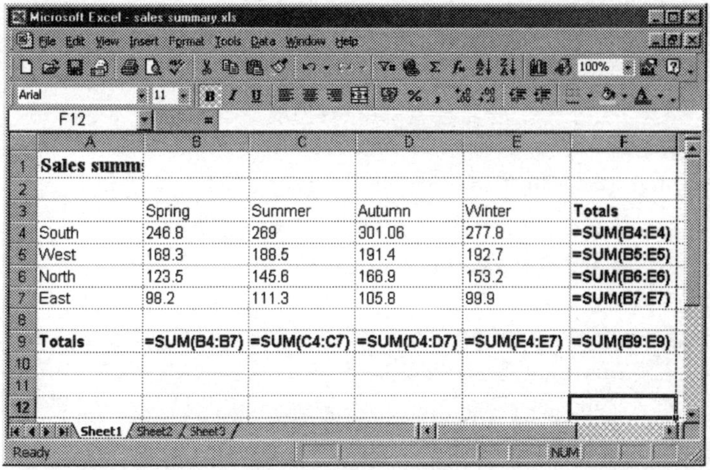

	A	B	C	D	E	F
1	**Sales summ**					
2						
3		Spring	Summer	Autumn	Winter	**Totals**
4	South	246.8	269	301.06	277.8	**=SUM(B4:E4)**
5	West	169.3	188.5	191.4	192.7	**=SUM(B5:E5)**
6	North	123.5	145.6	166.9	153.2	**=SUM(B6:E6)**
7	East	98.2	111.3	105.8	99.9	**=SUM(B7:E7)**
8						
9	**Totals**	**=SUM(B4:B7)**	**=SUM(C4:C7)**	**=SUM(D4:D7)**	**=SUM(E4:E7)**	**=SUM(B9:E9)**
10						
11						
12						

Figure 4.8 When Excel displays formulae, it makes the columns very wide – do not shrink them unless you have to. They will revert to their previous width when you hide the formulae again.

To hide formulae:

- Open the **Options** dialog box and clear the tick by **Formulas.**

4.9 Exercise

Spreadsheets are often used for testing 'What if?' scenarios. What if sales can be increased by 10% this year? What if our clients are slow payers? What if we invest in the new machinery? When will it pay for itself? What if we take on this project? How much do we need to borrow and when can we pay it back?

You can answer these questions without a spreadsheet, but it takes so long. With a spreadsheet, once you have set up the model, you can test out a whole range of possibilities in very little time. The hardest part is to create the model. To do this, you need to know how the different values are related to each other.

Here is the scenario for this exercise. You are planning to open a small store, and have come up with these figures.

- You can borrow 50,000 to get started.
- Your **running costs** will be 10,000 per month for wages, rent, heat and light, etc.

- The **cost of goods** is related to sales – assume that they are 50% of sales and that you pay for the goods in the same month that you sell them.
- Assume that sales start at 5,000 in the first month, then grow by 40% each month to a maximum of 75,000.

Use the spreadsheet to find the answers to these questions:

- How long will it be before you make a profit?
- When will the overdraft be cleared?

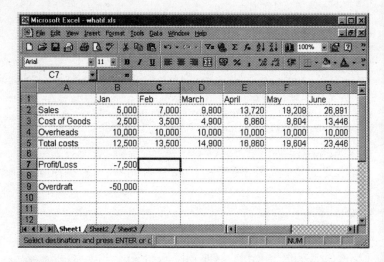

Figure 4.9 The spreadsheet at an early stage in its construction. At this point the sales, cost of goods and overheads have been entered or calculated. Use this as a guide to check that you are on the right path with your formulae.

Summary

- Spreadsheets have two layers – the formatted text and values that you can see on the screen, and the actual data and formulae that lie beneath.

- A cell can be identified by its column letter and row number. A range of cells can be identified by the references of the cells at opposite corners of the range.

- Data is entered and edited in the Formula bar.

- Formulae are written using arithmetic operators, working on actual values or values held in cells. They can also use functions – predefined calculations.

- Text can be formatted to change its font, size and style.

- Numbers can be formatted to suit the types of values which they represent.

- You can insert or delete rows and columns at any time, anywhere in the sheet. The width of columns and height of rows can be adjusted as required.

- Before printing, you should check the preview and adjust the page setup if necessary.

- If you want to print formulae, you need to turn on their display in the options.

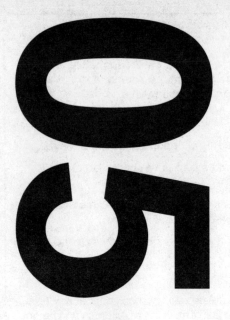

05

databases

In this chapter you will learn

- key concepts of databases
- how to enter and edit data
- how to sort records
- how to create queries
- how to print a data table

5.1 Key concepts

Database

A database is an organized set of data. It consists of the data itself, and the tools for getting information out of it. A database may be very simple, e.g. a list of names and addresses, with a means of producing mailing labels; or very complex, e.g. a school database could hold details of the pupils, staff and the lessons, and be used for producing class lists, timetables and details of any individual.

Database management system

This is an application that is used to manage a database. We will be using Access, from the Microsoft Office suite.

Tables

Data is stored in tables, organized by rows and columns. A database may have several tables, with each with a distinct set of data. A business database might, for instance, have a supplier table, a client table, an employee table and a stock table.

Each row contains a record, which has the data for one member of the table, e.g. for each client in a client database.

Each column represents a field, which holds the same kind of data for each record; e.g, in a client database, there would be a field for surnames, another for telephone numbers – amongst others.

Where a row and column meet, you have a cell, containing one field for one record.

Queries

Queries are used to select records, e.g. all the clients with overdue debts, or the students in class 3B. The query may contain the full details of each matching record, or just selected fields.

Forms

Forms are used for entering, editing and displaying data. A form will normally show the details of only one record at a time.

Reports

Reports are used to print information from a table or query, and may include summaries of the information in selected fields.

Field name   Fields

Client	Street	Town	Telephone
John Brown	24 Market Square	Newtown	010 123 6543
Mrs Pears	12 High Street	Newtown	010 123 4567
Reg	187 High Street	Newtown	010 123 4789

Records

Figure 5.1 In a database table, each row holds a record, each column holds a field.

In an Access database, all the tables, queries, reports and other elements are stored in a single file.

5.2 Microsoft Access

To start Access, click its Desktop icon, or select it from the **Start** menu – it will either be in the **Programs** menu or in a **Microsoft Office** submenu.

Microsoft Access

The Access screen

The layout of the screen depends upon the job that you are doing and how you choose to arrange the windows and toolbars.

The Database window

This is the control centre. Use it to create and open the tables, queries, forms and reports that make up the database. This has a different layout in Access 97, but is used in the same way.

Table window

Each table, query or other object is opened in its own window. These can be moved, minimized or resized as needed.

The Standard toolbar

This should be open all the time. It has tools for the most commonly-used tasks.

The Formatting toolbar

This opens automatically when you are designing forms and reports. It can be opened when working with tables, but note that

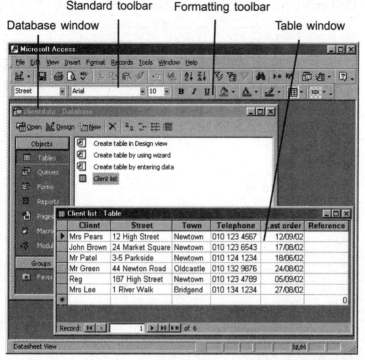

Standard toolbar   Formatting toolbar

Database window   Table window

Figure 5.2 The Access screen when a table is open. The Formatting toolbar is not normally displayed when you are working in a table, but can be turned on if required.

any formatting applies to the whole table – you cannot format selected cells, fields or records. This is because tables are really only intended for simple data entry and editing. If you need a neatly laid out screen for data entry, you can use a form; if you want a well-presented printout, you can use a report.

5.3 Creating a database

The first thing you must do is either create a new database or open an exisiting one. You do not have to know how to create a database for New CLAIT, but you do need one to experiment with. If you do not have a suitable database on your system – or if you simply want to know how to create a database – then follow these instructions. If sample data is available, skip to section 5.4.

The first job is to set up the overall database file to hold the tables, queries and reports that will be created later. The database must be named and saved before you can do anything else.

1 Start Access from the **Start** menu or the Desktop shortcut icon.

2 In the **Create a new database using** area of the Access start-up panel, choose **Blank Access database** and click **OK**.

◆ If Access is already running, use **File > New...** and double-click the Database icon.

3 At the **File New Database** dialog box, select the folder in which to store it.

4 In the **File name** box, enter the name. Access will add the extension of *.mdb*.

5 Click **Create**.

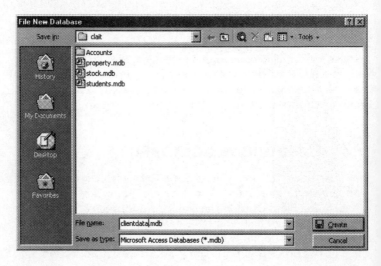

Creating a table

Access can handle different types of data, e.g. text, numbers and dates, and for each type there are options that allow you to specify exactly how it is stored. You can, for example, set the size of a text field. If you were setting up a database from scratch, you would expect to spend quite some time analysing your data to work out the best table structure for it. We're going to cheat, to save time.

Our sample database will hold details of a firm's clients. For each client it needs to hold this data:

> Client's name
>
> Address (Street and Town only)
>
> Telephone number
>
> Last order date

Except for the *Last order date*, the fields will hold text, and the default size of 50 characters will be more than enough.

To create a table:

1 At the Database window, select *Tables* in the **Objects** list and double-click **Create table in Design view**. The **Table Design** window will open.

For each field perform steps **2** and **3**:

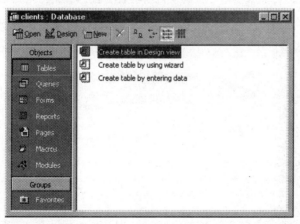

2 Type the **Field Name** and press [**Enter**].

3 The default data type is *Text* – this is what we want for the first four fields, so press [**Enter**]. When you get to the *Last Order* field, click the arrow and select *Date/Time* from the list.

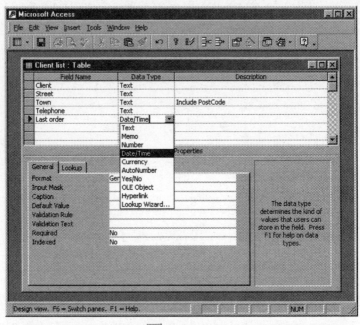

4 Click the **Save** button . You will be asked if you would like Access to set a Primary key. We don't need one, so say **No**.

5 Type a name for the table – call it *Client list* – and click **OK**.

You need some sample data for the table. Use the client list given on the next page, or make up your own clients. Entering the data will give you practice in the techniques covered in section 5.5!

Sample client data

Client	Street	Town	Telephone	Last order
Pearsons	12 High Street	Newtown	010 123 4567	12/09/02
Brown Bros	24 Market Square	Newtown	010 123 6543	17/08/02
Patel & Son	3-5 Parkside	Newtown	010 124 1234	18/06/02
Green's	44 Newton Road	Oldcastle	010 132 9876	24/08/02
Doe, Robert	187 High Street	Newtown	010 123 4789	05/09/02
Lee, Xang	1 River Walk	Bridgend	010 134 1234	27/08/02
Johnson	8 Treelined Ave	Woodford	010 145 9876	03/07/02

5.4 Opening a database

To open a database at startup:

1 At the **Access** dialog box, click **Open an existing file**.

2 Select a file from the list.

Or

3 Click **More Files...** and browse through your folders.

To open a database during a session:

4 Use **File > Open** or click the **Open Database** button 🖼.

5 Select the folder and file.

6 Click **Open**.

5.5 Data entry

First you must open the table! Tables can be opened in Datasheet view for data entry, or in Design view if you need to change their structure – adding, removing or redefining fields. We only need to work in Datasheet view.

To open a table in Datasheet view:

1 The Database window will be open. Select the **Tables** tab.

2 Double-click on the table.

Or

3 Select the table and click the Open button 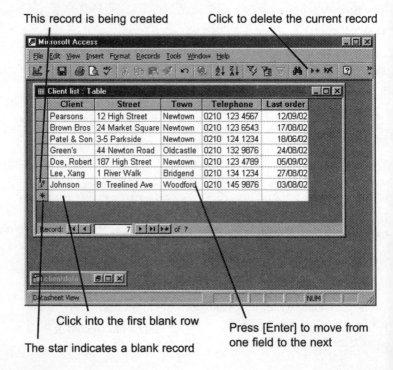 in the **Database** window.

In the Datasheet view, the columns are headed with the field names, and each row is a record. As you complete each record, it is automatically saved into the table and onto the disk file.

To enter data:

1 Click into the first blank row to start a new record.

2 Type the data into each field in turn and press [**Enter**] to move onto the next.

3 If you want to leave a field blank, simply press [**Enter**].

4 When you reach the end of the record, press [**Enter**] again to move on and start a new record.

This record is being created   Click to delete the current record

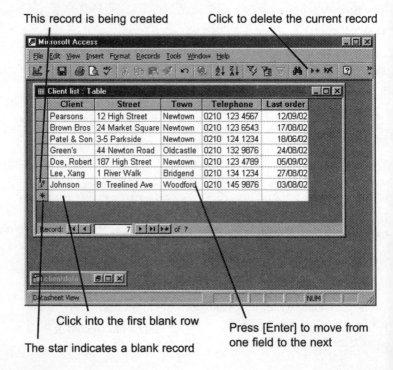

Click into the first blank row

The star indicates a blank record

Press [Enter] to move from one field to the next

5 When you have finished entering data, click the **Close** button ☒ to close the table – you do not need to save it as data is saved automatically as it is entered.

Entering dates

Access recognizes dates written in many formats. All these, for example, will be accepted:

3/8/02	3 Aug 2002
03-08-02	3 8 02

The default display format in the UK is **dd/mm/yy**, for example 03/08/02. This can be changed in Design view.

5.6 Editing data

Data can be edited, to correct mistakes or update entries. The text and figures can be changed, deleted or added to as in any other Windows application.

To edit the text in a field:

* Click into it or move to the cell and press [**F2**] to switch to edit mode. (See *Moving between records* below.)

To delete an unwanted record:

* Select it (see below) and click ☒ or use **Edit > Delete Record**. You will be prompted to confirm the deletion.

Moving between records

You can move through the records by using the **Edit > Go To** options, the [↑], [↓] arrow keys, [**Page Up**] and [**Page Down**], or the vertical scroll bar.

In a big database, the simplest way to move around is with the navigation buttons in the lower-left of the window.

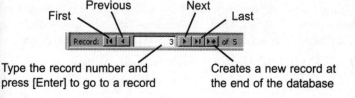

Type the record number and press [Enter] to go to a record

Creates a new record at the end of the database

Selecting data

When an area is selected, it appears in inverse colour, normally white on black.

To select	Do this
A single field	Point to the left-hand side of the field, so that the cursor changes to a cross, and click.
A word in a field	Double-click on the word.
A record	Click on the record selector on the left.
Several records	Either drag highlight down the record selectors to select a block, or hold [**Ctrl**] and click on the selectors one by one to select scattered records.
A column	Click on the name at the top of the column.

Click on the corner square to select all the data in the table

Click to select a record

Click on the left to select one cell

Click to select a field

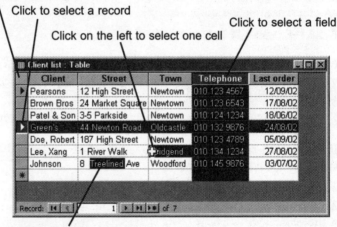

Double-click to select a word

Find and Replace

Finding a record in a large database can be difficult if you have to search though it 'by hand'. Fortunately, you do not! The **Find** routine will track down any records containing a given value.

You can restrict the search to a selected field, or look through the whole database. A restricted search is faster and more efficient.

To find records:

1 If you only want to search a certain field, select it first.

2 Open the **Edit** menu and select **Find...** or click 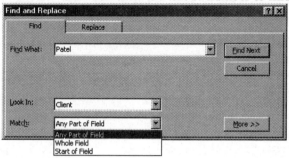 the **Find** button on the Standard toolbar.

3 In the **Find What** box enter the text or number to find.

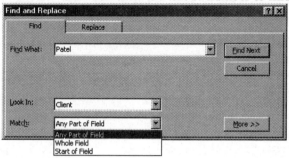

4 For a restricted search, set the **Look In** box to the field name, otherwise this should be set to the whole table.

5 In the **Match** box, select the part or whole of the field to be matched.

6 Click **Find Next**. The first matching record will be displayed.

7 If the record is not the one you want, click **Find Next** again.

8 When you have done, click 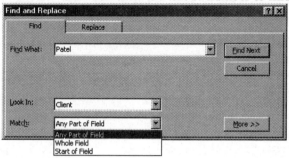 to close the dialog box.

Replace

If you need to make the same change to a number of records, you can do this quickly using **Replace**.

1 Open the **Edit** menu and select **Replace...**

2 Type the original text or value in the **Find What** box.

3 Type the new text or value in the **Replace With** box.

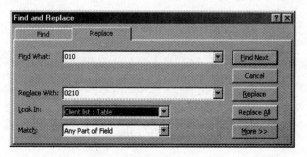

4 Set the **Look In** and **Match** options as for **Find**.

5 Click **Find Next** to locate the first matching record, and then **Replace** to make the change. Repeat to work through all the changes individually, checking as you go.

6 If you are sure that the replacement will only affect the entries that you want to change, click **Replace All**.

5.7 Sorting records

Records are normally displayed in the order in which they were entered. They can be sorted into order on any field. The sort can be ascending or descending, and will be in alphabetic, numeric or date order, depending upon the values in the field.

* *Sorting on a column will bring together those records with the same value in that field, e.g. those in the same town. They can then be selected as a group.*

To change the displayed order:

1 Click the field name of the column by which you wish to sort.

2 Click the ⬆ **Sort Ascending** or ⬇ **Sort Descending** button.

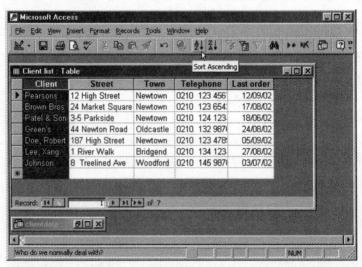

Figure 5.3 This will sort the database by ascending alphabetical order of clients. Sorting on the Last order field would put the records in (ascending or descending) date order.

To restore the original order:

3 Open the **Records** menu and select **Remove Filter/Sort**.

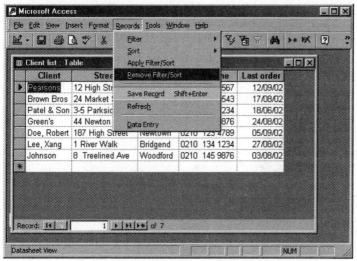

Figure 5.4 When the sort is removed, the database reverts to its natural order – the order in which records were entered.

5.8 Simple queries

The information in a database is of no use unless it can be retrieved quickly and in a useful form. Queries allow you to search for and retrieve specific records, e.g. clients with overdue bills. The selected set can then be printed if needed (see page 140).

Queries may be based on more than one table, but here all the queries will be based on a single *Client list* table.

There are two aspects to designing a query:

- Selecting the *fields* to be shown in the query. You do not normally need all the fields, for example you would only want names and addressses for a mailshot.

- Selecting the *records* to be included. Access allows you to set up a query by describing the data that you are looking for.

You can create a query by using a wizard or in Design view. The wizard is simple to use, but limited – it can be used to select fields, but not to select records. Without further work, a wizard query would list all the records in the table. However, a query started here can be modified in the Query Design window, and it is simpler to do this than to start from scratch in Design view.

1 At the Database window, click on the **Queries** tab and double-click on **Create query by using wizard**. In Access 97, click New to get the wizard options.

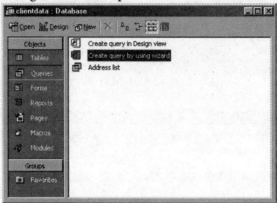

2 Select each of the fields you want to show, from the **Available Fields** list and click ▶ to add them to the **Selected Fields** list.

To add all the fields, click ▶▶.

If you add fields by mistake, click ◀, or click ◀◀ to remove all the fields and start again.

3 Click **Next**.

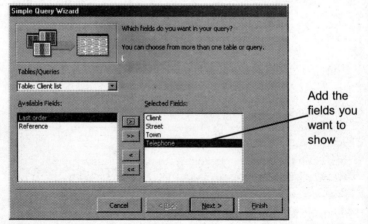

Add the fields you want to show

4 Give the query a title.

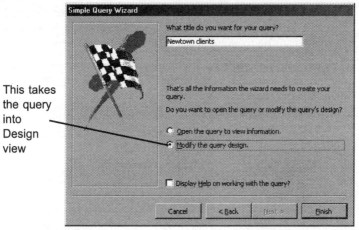

This takes the query into Design view

5 Select **Modify the query design** and click **Finish**. The Query Design window will open.

The Query Design window

Fields can be added to the query by double-clicking on them in the list. This is how to select them in Access 97.

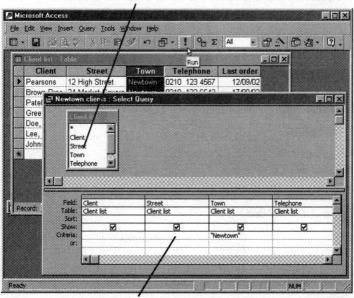

If ticked, the field will be shown in the results. If you want to set criteria on a field, but not show that field in the output, clear the **Show** tick.

In the Query Design window you can define how to select records, by writing into the **Criteria** what you want to find in that field. If you write in a value, only records with matching data are selected.

1 Click into the **Criteria** cell of the field on which you want to select, and enter the value that must be matched, e.g. the name of a town in the *Town* field.

2 Click ⚡ the **Run** button.

The resulting set will be displayed. This shows the selected fields for those records that match the criteria.

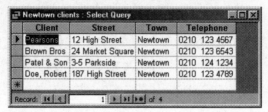

3 After viewing the results, click ⊠ to close the display. You will be prompted to save the changes that you have made to the query – click **Yes**.

The query is saved as part of the database. It will be listed by name in the Query area of the Database window and can be reopened from there if you need to run it again in the future.

5.9   Queries using operators

Simply entering a value for the Criteria cell will only find exact matches. Very often you want those that fall into a range, e.g. customers owing more than a certain amount. To find these we can use the *relational operators*.

Operator	Meaning
>	Greater than
<	Less than
<>	Not equal to
>=	Greater than or equal to
<=	Less than or equal to

These can be used on any type of value, not just numeric, e.g. '<=M' in a *Surname* field would match those people whose surname began with anything from 'A' to 'M'. '>30/08/02' will find any dates after the end of August 2002.

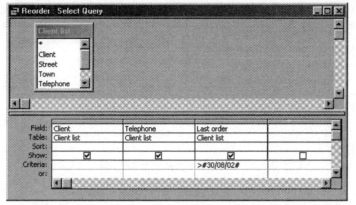

Figure 5.5 Access will accept dates in a range of formats (see page 131). They will be converted to the standard dd/mm/yy format and enclosed in hashes. Text values have quotes added.

AND and OR queries

A query may have several criteria.

If two or more criteria must be met, then you have a logical AND. For example, in a student database, to find students who were over 16 AND played football, you would set '>16' as the criterion in the *Age* field and 'Football' in the *Sports* field. Both criteria must be true for the record to be retrieved.

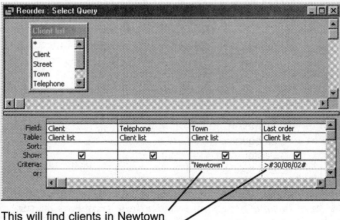

This will find clients in Newtown
whose last order was after 30/08/02

AND can be used to set several criteria in a single field, e.g. clients whose last order was after 1/7/02 AND before 31/7/02. You could select these by writing '>1/7/02 AND <31/7/02' in the Criteria cell of the *Last order* field.

If either two or more alternative values may be matched, you have a logical OR. For example, you could create a query to select clients in Oldcastle or Bridgend. Notice the **or:** row in the query design grid. To set up OR queries, write the first value in the Criteria cell, then the alternative value in the **or:** cell of the same field.

This finds clients in Newtown or Bridgend – other alternatives could be added on more rows below

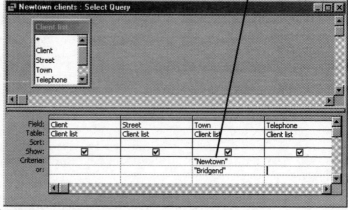

5.10 Printing from Access

There are two ways to get printouts from a database – you can print from reports or directly from tables.

Report-based printouts can be formatted and the data organized and summarized in a number of ways, but reports are not that simple to set up. Nor are they part of the New CLAIT syllabus!

Table-based printouts are a crude but effective means of getting your data onto paper. The table is printed as it appears on the datasheet, and for all but the smallest tables, the printout will be too large to fit on one sheet of paper. Instead it will be spread over several pages, working across from left to right, then from top to bottom. For example, if a table is two pages wide and three long, Access will print the top two pages first, i.e. all the fields of the first set of records, then the next two pages and finally the bottom two.

If you only want to print out certain records, there are two ways to do this – either select the records from within the table (see page 132) or run a query (see page 135). The table resulting from a query can be printed in exactly the same way as a data table.

To print from a table:

1 Display the table in Datasheet view.
2 If you only want to print certain records, select them now.
3 From the **File** menu, select **Print Preview** and check the layout and page breaks.
4 Open the **File** menu and select **Print...**
5 Under the **Print Range** choose:
   All, to print the whole table.
   Pages, to print specific pages – specifiy the numbers of the first and last pages.
   Selected Records, if you selected some at **2**.
6 Set the other options as required.
7 Click **OK**.

What do you want to print?

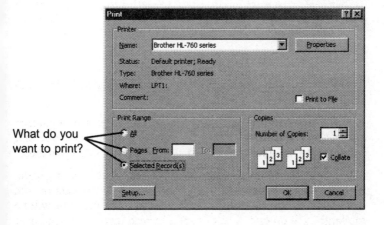

5.11 Saving and closing

Access automatically saves the data in a database regularly during a session and when it is closed. Access is different from the other Office applications in this respect. The reason for this is that a database is designed to be run from the disk, rather than from memory – other documents are stored in memory while they are being worked on. Holding the active data on the disk has two important advantages – it allows the file to be very large (and some Access databases are enormous!) and it allows a number of people to be working on the same data at the same time.

You will not normally need to use a **File > Save** command. You may sometimes be asked if you want to save the *design* of a table – if, for example, you have sorted it.

To close a table:

1 Click the table's ▨ **Close** button.

Or

2 Use **File > Close**.

♦ If you have changed its design or layout in any way, you will be asked if you want to save it. Your data is safe whether you save the design changes or not.

To close a database:

1 Close any open tables.

2 Click the Database window's ▨ **Close** button.

Or

3 Use **File > Close**.

5.12 Exercise

1 Open the *client* database.

2 Open the client table.

3 Make the following additions and corrections to the data:

Add a new client: Mr Singh, 5 Park View, Oldcastle, Tel 010 132 8760, First (and last) order was today.

Mrs Pears, Mr Patel and Ms Brown have also placed orders today.

Delete Mr Green

Mrs Lee has moved to 19 River Walk

The telephone numbers have been reorganized. All 010 numbers should now start 0210

4 Sort the table into descending order of the *Last order* field.

5 Print one copy of the table.

6 Create a query to show those clients who are not in Newtown (use the <> operator), including the *Client, Street, Town* and *Telephone* fields.

7 Print the table produced by the query.

8 Close the database and exit from Access.

Summary

* A database consists of tables of data and tools, such as queries and reports, for getting information from it.

* Databases are opened from the Access start-up panel or the File menu. Tables and other objects are opened from the Database window.

* To enter a new record, go to the bottom of the table and type the data into the blank row that you'll find there.

* To edit a record, navigate to it, then press [**F2**] or click into the cell you want to change.

* The Find routine will locate records quickly. If you need to make the same change many times, you should use the Replace routine.

* Records can be sorted into ascending or descending order of the values in any chosen field.

* Queries enable you to get information from your database. You can select which fields to include, and specify one or more criteria to select records.

* When printing tables, you should preview them first to see how they will fit onto the paper.

* Data is saved automatically as it is entered. Design changes are only saved if you choose.

06 desktop publishing

In this chapter you will learn

- about DTP programs and word processors
- how to use frames
- how to format text
- how to use templates
- how to insert images and clip art
- how to print a document

6.1 DTP and word processing

Until a few years ago, DTP (desktop publishing) and word processing were two distinct things.

- DTP was concerned with the layout of varied text and images to produce books, magazines, brochures and the like. The software typically had limited text-editing facilities – enough to correct errors and type in captions – but no spell checking.

- Word processing software allowed you to create and edit text, and was used for producing letters, memos, reports and other text where limited formatting was enough. The only control over layout was through the margins, the alignment options – and blank lines! In the early days, when computer printers had a single fixed set of keys, you couldn't even change the size or type of font.

Applications of each type have improved steadily over the years and had more and more of each other's facilities added to them, so that current DTP and word processing applications can very largely do each other's jobs. This book is being written directly in PageMaker, a DTP package. Word is used to produce newsletters, brochures and other highly formatted documents – it is even used by some professional typesetters to create books.

In this chapter we will be using Publisher, the DTP software in the Microsoft Office suite.

6.2 Microsoft Publisher

When Publisher starts, it offers you a selection of wizards, designs and blank documents. The wizards and designs are well worth exploring at some point as they let you create quite professional publications with relatively little effort. However, we will start with a blank document, as we need to know how things work!

The screen display is similar to that of Word, but notice the top set of buttons in the Objects toolbar on the left of the window. These are used for creating *frames*. In Publisher, text, images and other material are placed in frames, not directly on the page (see page 150).

The Publisher screen

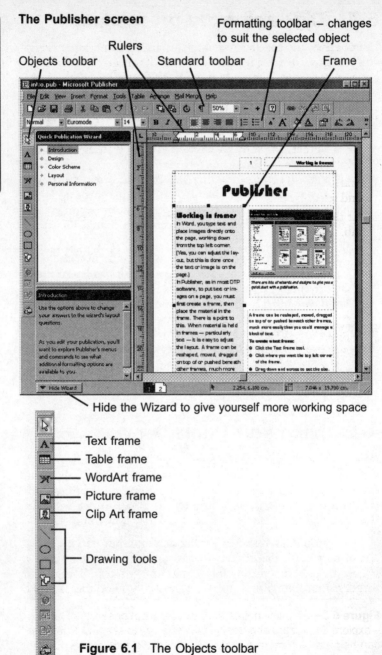

Objects toolbar
Rulers
Standard toolbar
Formatting toolbar – changes to suit the selected object
Frame

Hide the Wizard to give yourself more working space

Text frame
Table frame
WordArt frame
Picture frame
Clip Art frame

Drawing tools

Figure 6.1 The Objects toolbar

6.3 Page setup

In Publisher, the page setup depends mainly on the paper size – you can have anything from tiny business cards up to multi-sheet banners or posters. The paper size is normally defined at the start, by selecting from the Catalog.

If there is no suitable blank publication, there are more paper sizes, including labels and envelopes in the **Page Setup** dialog box. You can also use this to change the paper size, after starting work on a publication.

1 Start Publisher, or if it is already running, open the **File** menu and select **New**.

2 At the **Catalog** dialog box, switch to the **Blank Publications** tab.

3 Select a size and fold, either from the list on the left or the icons in the main display.

4 If you want to select a size from the **Page Setup** dialog box (Figure 6.3), click **Custom Page...**

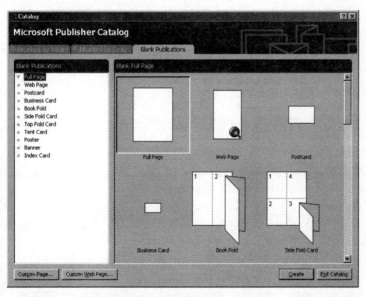

Figure 6.2 All publications start from the options in the Catalog – explore the Wizard and Design tabs one day to see how Publisher can help you to create a professional-looking publication quickly.

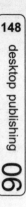

Pick a size...

...or define
your own size

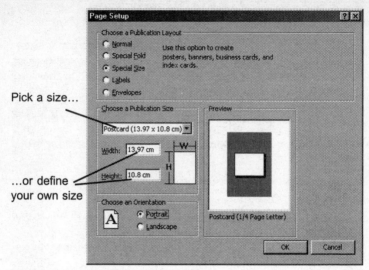

Figure 6.3 The Page Setup dialog box. The options vary with
the layout. The Orientation can change the shape of folded and
larger publications, but does not matter with small ones.

5 If you want to change the size after starting a publication, use
File > Page Setup to open the **Page Setup** dialog box.

6.4 Layout

You can place anything anywhere (in a frame) on a Publisher page,
but you normally want all the pages of a publication to have the
same basic shape, and the layout guides are there to help with this.

There are two aspects to layout – margins and columns. Both can
be set through the **Layout Guides** dialog box.

The *margin* settings are the distances between the edges of the
paper (as defined by the Paper Size, not the actual sheet that you
will print on) and the start of the working area.

The grid guides can be used to divide the page into any number
of columns or rows. Two- or three-column formats are often used
for newsletters and brochures. Row guides, or row and column
guides together, can be useful when setting up a page of images or
other small, regular items.

To set the page layout:

1 Open the **Arrange** menu and select **Layout Guides…**

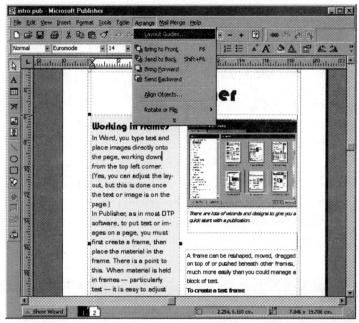

2 Set the margins by typing new values, or by clicking the little arrows on the right.

3 To divide the page into columns (or rows), set the numbers in the **Grid guides** area.

4 Click **OK**.

These are only guides. When you place the frames (see the next pages), they can overlap or fit inside the guides as required to create larger or smaller margins or gaps between columns.

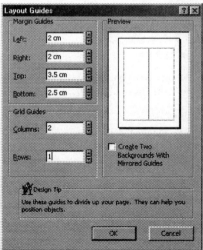

6.5 Working in frames

In Word, you type text and place images directly onto the page, working down from the top left corner. (Yes, you can adjust the layout, but this is done once the text or image is on the page.)

In Publisher, as in most DTP software, to put text or images on a page, you first create a frame, then place the material in the frame. There is a point to this. When material – particularly text – is held in frames, it is easy to adjust the layout. A frame can be reshaped, moved, dragged on top of or pushed beneath other frames, much more easily than you could manage a block of text.

To create a text frame:

1 Click the **Text frame** tool.
2 Click where you want the top left corner of the frame.
3 Drag down and across to set the size.
4 The text cursor will be waiting at the top left – type your text.

Text frame tool

Type at the cursor

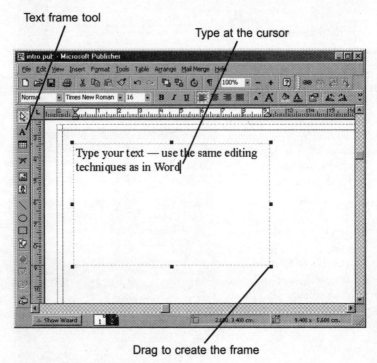

Drag to create the frame

Managing frames

A frame can be moved or resized at any time, before or after its
text or image is added. Resizing is the same for all frames. Moving
is slightly different in text and picture or clip art frames.

To resize a frame:

1   Click into the frame to select it, so that the handles appear at
the corners and sides.

2   Point to a handle – the cursor will change to this icon. ⬚ᴿᴱˢᴵᶻᴱ.
Click on the handle and drag to change the size and shape of
the frame.

To move a text frame:

◆   Point to the dotted line on any edge of the frame. The cursor
will change to ⬚ᴹᴼⱽᴱ. Click and drag the frame to its new place.

To move a picture or clip art frame:

◆   Move the cursor anywhere over the frame. The cursor will
change to ⬚ᴹᴼⱽᴱ. Click and drag the frame to its new place.

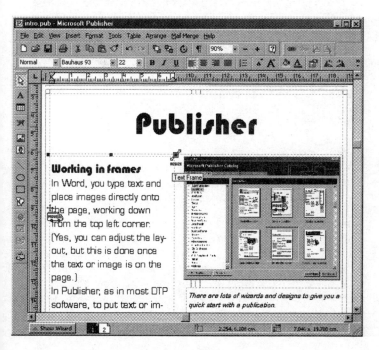

6.6 Formatting text

In Publisher you have almost the same formatting tools as in Word – the font type, size and colour, emphasis and alignment options are exactly the same. You also have a few extra tools.

- **Decrease font size** takes the selected text to the next size down in the Font size list.
- **Increase font size** takes the selected text to the next size up.
- **Fill Color** sets the background colour of the frame that the cursor is in.
- **Text frame properties** opens a dialog box where you can set the internal margins for the frame and other properties.
- **Rotate left** turns the frame 90° to the left around its centre.
- **Rotate right** turns the frame 90° to the right.

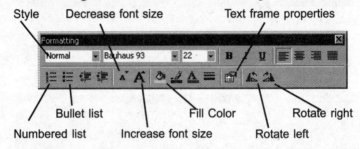

Style Decrease font size Text frame properties

Bullet list Fill Color Rotate right

Numbered list Increase font size Rotate left

Figure 6.4 The Formatting toolbar, seen here in its 'floating' form rather than docked at the top of the screen. The unlabelled tools are the same as in Word.

6.7 Styles

A *style* is a named set of formatting options. Using styles allows you to format your text faster and ensures consistency.

Suppose that you wanted all your main headings to be Arial, 14pt, bold, with a 6pt space above. To format every heading like this will take at least four operations each time. If you defined those options into a style, called perhaps *Heading 1*, you could format your headings by simply selecting the style from the list. And, even better, if you decide you want to make all the headings larger or use a different font, you can change them all by simply redefining the style.

To create a style:

1 Open the **Format** menu and select **Text Style…**

2 Click the  button beside **Create a new style**.

To change an existing style,
select it then click this button

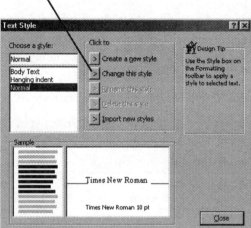

The Sample
shows what the
font looks like and
the shape and
spacing of lines in
the paragraph

3 At the **Create New Style** dialog box, enter a name for your new style.

4 Click the ≥ button beside **Character type and size**.

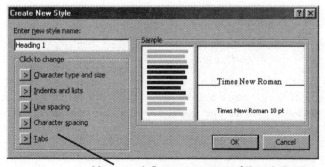

You can define any aspect of the character
formatting and the paragraph layout from here

5 Define the font, size, style and colour, and set any effects as required, using the **Sample** display as a guide.

6 Click **OK** to return to the **Create New Style** dialog box.

7 Click the ▷ button beside any other aspect you want to define – for headings, you should set the spacing.

8 Spacing is defined in points. As a guide, the default *Normal* style is 12pt, so a 24pt space is equivalent to two lines. Experiment with these settings and see how they look – remember that you can come back and adjust them at any time.

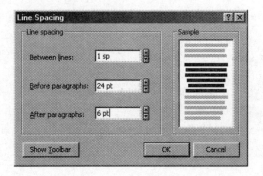

To edit a style:

◆ Follow the steps for creating a style, but at step 2 select the style you want to edit and click  beside **Change this style**.

To apply a style:

1 Click anywhere in the paragraph, or drag the highlight over the set of paragraphs that you want to format.

2 Drop down the style list and select the style.

◆ Styles can only be applied to whole paragraphs. If you want to vary the size, font or style of text within a paragraph, you must set the format options one at a time.

6.8   The background

There are two levels to every publication – the foreground and the background.

◆ The foreground is different for every page. This is where you normally work.

◆ The background acts as a 'master' for the whole publication. Anything placed on the background is displayed on every page. If you want page numbers, logos or titles in a publication, this is where they go.

To add page numbers:

1 Open the **View** menu and select **Go to Background**.

2 Draw a text frame where you want the number, e.g. in the top or bottom margin.

3 Open the **Insert** menu and select **Page Numbers**. A hash (#) will be inserted.

4 Format the page number as you would format any text.

5 Open the **View** menu and select **Go to Foreground**. At this level, the hash is replaced by the correct number for the page – and if you insert more pages, or delete them, the numbers will be automatically adjusted.

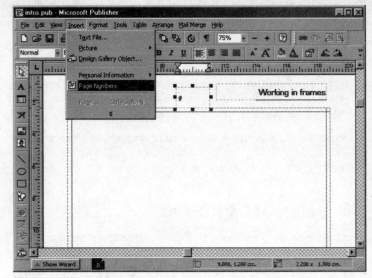

Figure 6.5 Adding page numbers to the background. Notice the title 'Working in frames' on the top right. This text, and the line drawn underneath it will be shown on every page.

6.9 Templates and wizards

Publisher is supplied with a large selection of designs for a wide range of publications. If you want to produce a good-looking publication quickly, start from one of these templates. Each consists of a layout of frames, with prompts to show what text or images are to go in each frame; it also has the fonts and sizes defined for its text styles, plus a background and other decorative graphics. When you first open the template, a wizard will help you to customize it to your requirements.

The templates are opened from the Publisher Catalog, where they are organized in two ways. On the **Publications by Wizard** tab, they are grouped by type of publication – if you are creating a single, stand-alone document, it is simplest to start from here; on the **Publications by Design** tab they are grouped by design – start from this tab when you are creating a number of publications and want to use the same design for them all.

To use a template:

1 Open the **File** menu and select **New**.

2 Open the **Publications by Wizard** tab and select the type of publication, then the design.

Or

3 On the **Publications by Design** tab, pick the design then the type.

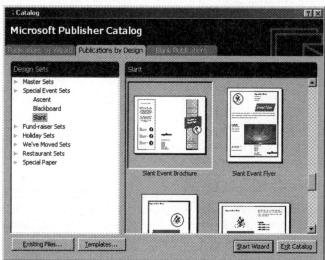

4 Set the colour scheme and other options through the Wizard, clicking **Next** at each step and **Finish** at the end.

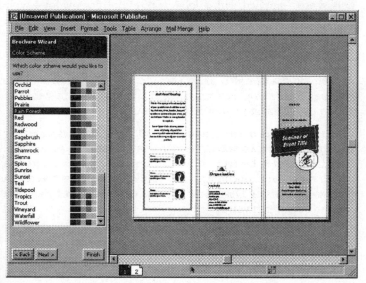

5 Go through the publication, replacing the prompts with your own text or images. Any unwanted elements can be selected and deleted. If you need extra text frames, copy an existing one rather than start from scratch, to ensure that the font styles are consistent.

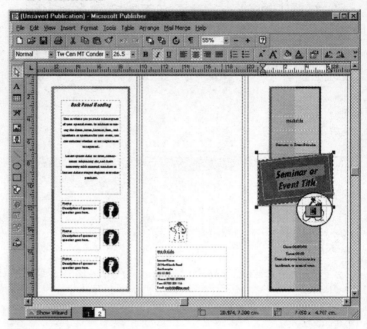

Custom templates

Starting from a template is quicker than starting from a blank document, but it can be even quicker if it is already customized with your information and preferences.

The trick is to save the publication *after* you have entered the permanent information, e.g. your name and address on headed paper, but *before* you have entered the specific text, such as the text of the letter. If you select the *Publisher Template* type, Publisher will automatically open the *Templates* folder to save it in.

When you want to start a new publication based on one of these templates, click the **Templates** button at the bottom of the Catalog dialog box to open the *Templates* folder.

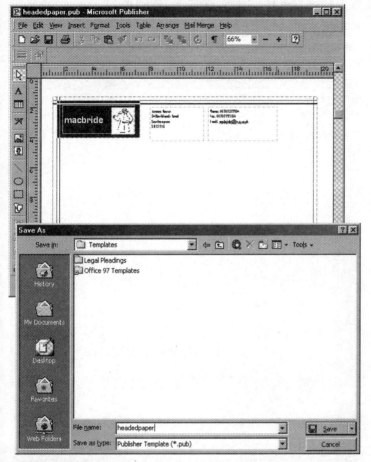

Figure 6.6 A template is simply a publication with the basic design and information in place. Storing it in the *Templates* folder allows Publisher to keep track of it.

The choice of folder is, in fact, the only difference between a template and a normal file in Publisher. When you start from one of these templates, you must remember to save it in a different folder, or with a different name, or the new publication will overwrite the template.

6.10 Working with images

Publisher can handle images in all the popular file formats, including bitmap (.bmp), Graphics Interchange Format (.gif), Joint Photographics Expert Group (.jpeg or .jpg), Kodak Photo CD (.pcd) and Windows Metafile (.wmf).

To place an image from a file:

1 Click the **Picture Frame** tool.

2 Click and drag to draw the frame.

3 Double-click in the frame to open the **Insert Picture** dialog box.

4 Work your way through to the right folder.

5 Select the picture.

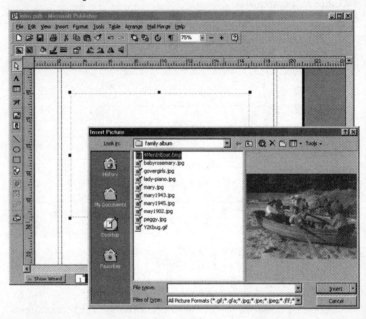

6 Click **Insert**.

7 Resize or move the image (see page 151) as necessary to fit into the layout.

◆ Images can be cropped or formatted using the tools on the Picture toolbar (see Section 8.10).

Clip art (Office 97)

Once clip art has been placed in a publication, it can be handled just like a picture. The only difference is in how it is inserted in the first place – instead of opening a file, you get clip art from the Clip Gallery, and the Clip Gallery is one of the few aspects of Microsoft Office that has changed between 97 and 2000.

Here is how it works in Office 97.

1 Click on the **Clip Gallery Frame** tool ![icon] and draw a frame on your page.

2 Double-click in the new frame. The **Clip Gallery** dialog box will open.

3 Select the **Clip Art** tab.

4 Choose a **Category**.

5 Scroll through and select a picture.

6 Click **Insert**.

Figure 6.7 The Clip Gallery in Office 97. If there are a lot of clips in a category, or you don't know which category to look in, click the Find button and enter one or more keywords to get a selection of images.

Clip art (Office 2000)

In Office 2000, clip art and pictures are stored together in the Gallery, and there are many more of both! The layout has been redesigned to give more space for the images, but this is used in almost exactly the same way as the old Gallery.

1 Click on the **Clip Gallery Frame** tool [image] and draw a frame on your page.

2 Double-click in the new frame. The **Clip Gallery** dialog box will open.

3 On the **Pictures** tab choose a **Category**.

Or

4 Type a **Search** word and press [**Enter**].

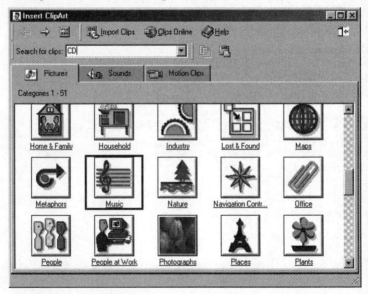

5 Click on a picture.

6 Click:

    to insert it;

    to preview it;

    to add it to your Favorites;

    to find similar clips.

7 Close the Gallery.

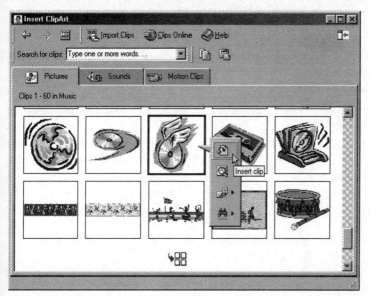

Figure 6.8 Inserting a clip from the Clip Gallery in Office 2000. Audio and video clips can also be inserted from here.

6.11 Lines and borders

Lines can be added around any frame – text, image or whatever – to make it stand out or to separate it from other material on the same page. The lines can form a complete border, or just be on selected sides; they can be solid lines of any thickness, or decorative borders of clip art.

• There is no option that will let you put a border around a whole page – but there is a way to achieve the same effect. You can create a frame that fills the page and add lines to that. (The frame will initially hide any others that are there already – use **Arrange > Send to Back** to push it behind the others.)

To add lines to a frame:

1 Select the frame.

2 Click the **Line/Border Style** tool.

3 For a simple black line, just select a thickness from the drop-down list.

Or

4 For anything else click **More Styles...**

5 For a line on one or more sides, go to the **Line Border** tab.

6 To set all the sides the same, simply choose a thickness.

7 To set sides individually, select a side then choose a thickness.

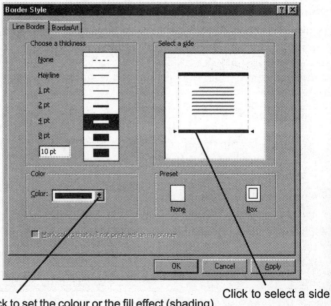

Click to set the colour or the fill effect (shading)

Click to select a side

8 For a decorative border, switch to the **BorderArt** tab.

9 Select a border from the list.

10 Click **OK** to close the dialog box.

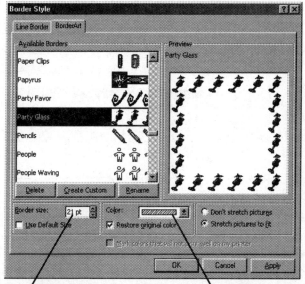

You can change the size...   ... or the colour

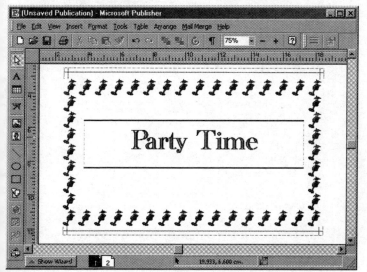

Figure 6.9 Two simple examples of lines and borders.

6.12 Printing

Printing is straightforward, but before you print, you should check your publication to make sure that the pages look the way you want them.

1 Click **−** to zoom out so that you can see the whole page.
2 Click **+** to zoom in and check details.
3 Click the page icons to move between the pages.

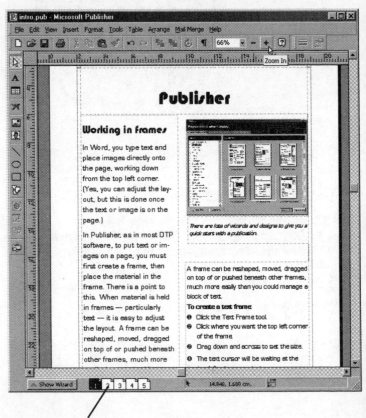

Click to change pages

4 Edit and adjust the layout until you are happy with the results. Then you are ready to print.
5 Open the **File** menu and select **Print**.

6 Set the **Print range** and **Number of copies.**

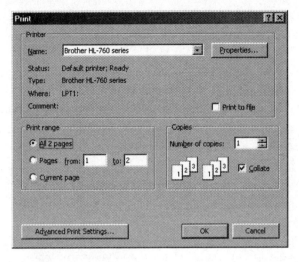

7 Click **OK** to start printing.

6.13 Exercise

A new restaurant, *Food for Thought,* has asked you to produce headed paper, menu/advertising brochures and business cards. They should follow the same basic design and have the same font and colour settings.

As you have not been given the menus, or other details of the business, you cannot take the publications through to finished products at this stage.

Starting from blank publications, create drafts to show the basic designs and concept.

Summary

- DTP software is used for laying out and formatting text and images to create books, brochures, newsletters, flyers and other publications.

- Publisher is the DTP program in Microsoft Office.

- The basic shape of a publication is set in the Page Setup.

- Text, images and other objects can be placed anywhere on the page in a publication, but must be in a *frame*.

- Text can be formatted in the same way as in Word. Text styles can ensure consistency in formatting.

- Text and objects placed on the background are visible on all pages.

- Templates are ready-made designs and layouts. Many are supplied with Publisher, and you can create your own easily.

- The wizards can help you to set up your publications.

- Images from file or from the Clip Gallery can be inserted into a page. They can be resized or moved as needed.

- Simple lines or decorative borders can be added around any frame.

- Before printing, check all your pages carefully.

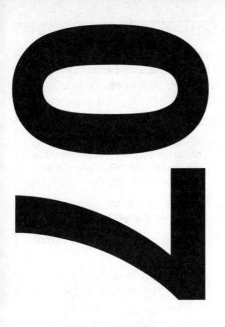

07

graphs and charts

In this chapter you will learn

- about different types of charts
- how to convert data into bar charts, line graphs and pie charts
- how to print a chart from Excel
- about Microsoft Graph

7.1 Getting meaning from numbers

Graphs and charts can bring out the meaning from sets of figures. They can show changes over time, variations between departments, the relative contribution that the parts make to a whole, and other relationships between numbers, and they can show them far more clearly than they can be seen in the raw data.

There are different types of graphs, designed to bring out different kinds of relationships between numbers. We will look at three commonly used types: bar charts, line graphs and pie charts.

Bar charts

Bar charts are good for comparing several sets, or *series*, of data – and especially for comparing the figures at the same point in the series. In this example, you can see how South's sales are so much higher than the other regions, in every quarter.

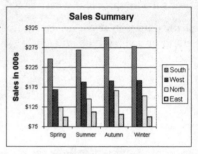

Line graphs

Line graphs are used for comparing several series, where you want to show changes over time. Here, for example, we can see how West's sales have increased steadily throughout the year, and have held up in the Winter, when the other regions all showed a drop.

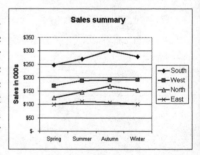

Pie charts

A pie chart can only display one series at a time, but it does show the relative contribution of each figure to the total. Here we can see that South's sales are almost as great as North and West's together.

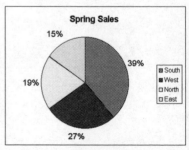

There are charting facilities in all Microsoft Office applications. The most comprehensive facilities are in Excel, and they are always present. In the other applications, you have to start by inserting a chart. We will concentrate on Excel.

7.2 Charting data

If the data that you want to chart is organized properly in the first place, then creating a chart is simple. If the data is not organized, the job will take a little longer, but is still not difficult. Ideally, the data should be in a continuous block – no unwanted rows or columns in the middle – with headings above and to the side.

If the data is in rows, i.e. each row will be displayed as a line on a graph or a set of bars on a chart, the top headings will be used to label the bottom axis of the chart, and the side headings will identify the rows in the legend. Where the data is in columns, the headings will be used the other way round.

With data in this form, you can simply run the Chart Wizard, which will collect a few choices from you and create the graph.

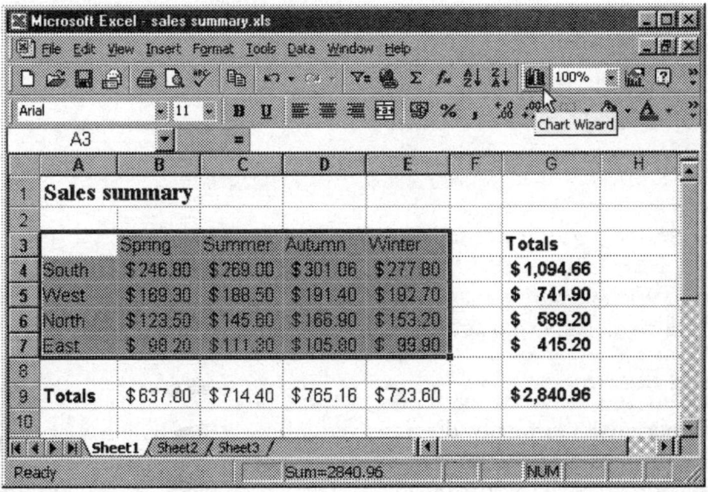

Figure 7.1 Here, each row of numbers will be used as a data series in the graph; the row headings will be used as labels in the legend and the top headings as labels for the X (horizontal) axis.

7.3 Creating a bar chart

For this exercise you need suitable sample data. You could use the spreadsheet shown in Figure 7.1 – only the range from A3 to E7 is needed for graphing.

1 Select the data, along with the headers.

2 Click the **Chart Wizard** tool 📊.

3 For the **Chart Type**, select *Column* – this has vertical bars; the *Bar* type has horizontal bars. Click on a **sub-type** then click **Next**.

Shows the name and description of the selected sub-type

4 At Step 2, check the **Data range**. Click 📊 if you need to re-define the range – you will be taken back into the sheet to select the data block.

5 Check the **Series in** setting – the Sales Summary figures are in *Rows*. Click **Next**.

6 At Step 3, go to the **Titles** tab and enter the **Chart title** and **Axis** labels. The options on the other tabs can be left at the defaults – but explore them to see what is available.

7 At Step 4, select where the chart is to go – as a new sheet or as an object in an existing sheet. Place the chart in the same sheet as the data if you want to be able to print both on the same piece of paper.

8 Click **Finish**.

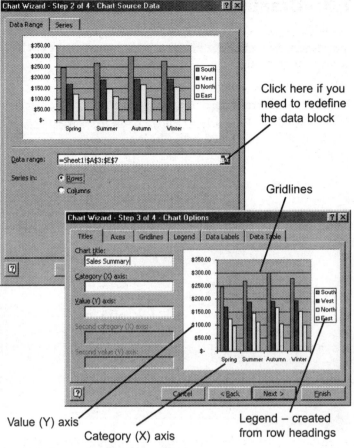

Click here if you need to redefine the data block

Gridlines

Value (Y) axis

Category (X) axis

Legend – created from row headings

Axes labels are not necessary if their meaning is obvious – e.g. 'time' or 'value'

Place the chart in the sheet if you want to print it with its data

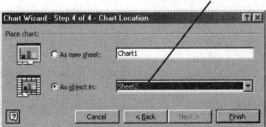

9 If the chart is placed in a sheet, the Wizard will drop it into the middle – drag it into place and resize it.

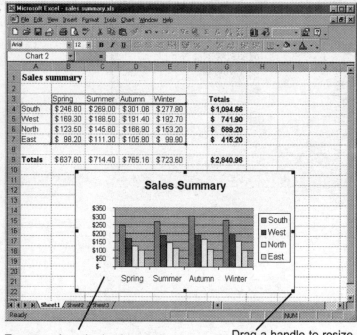

To move, drag the background – not an object, or you will move it within the chart!

Drag a handle to resize

7.4 Line graphs

A line graph can be created from scratch in exactly the same way as a bar chart, but selecting a different type at Step 1. However, we can also change the type of an existing chart – and that is what we will do now. The same data can be displayed as a bar chart or a line graph – and sometimes switching from one to the other will bring out different aspects of the figures.

After changing the type we will add a heading on the Y axis and adjust the Y axis scale.

1 Right-click the main chart area or open the **Chart** menu, and select **Chart Type…**

2 Select *Line* as the **Type**, and *Line* or *Line with markers* as the **sub-type**.

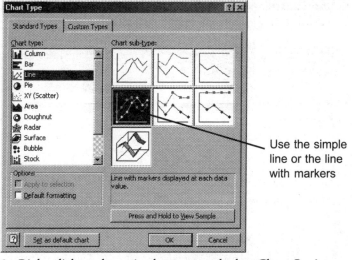

3 Right-click on the main chart area and select **Chart Options…**

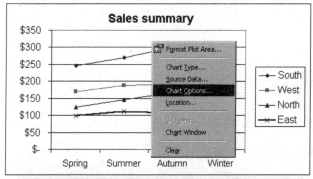

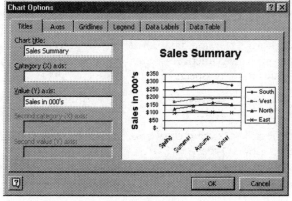

Use the simple line or the line with markers

4 On the **Title** tab, type 'Sales in 000's' in the **Value (Y) axis** field.

Excel automatically sets the Y axis scale to suit the values, normally starting from 0. If the values are all high, the lines will be cramped together at the top of the chart. We can define our own scale.

5 Right-click on the figures or the line of the Y axis and select **Format Axis...**

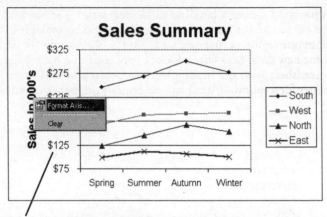

These have been formatted to show 0 decimal places – use the **Font** and **Number** tabs to change the appearance of the values

Define the scale to suit the range of values

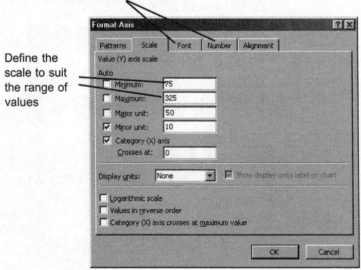

6 Open the **Scale** tab.

7 Type a suitable **Minimum** value.

8 Adjust the **Maximum** value if you want to change the space at the top of the chart.

9 Click **OK** to close the dialog box.

7.5 Pie charts

A pie chart can only handle a single data series. For our example, we could use the same Sales Summary figures, making a chart from one region or one quarter at a time, but perhaps it's time for some new data. Let's have a look at your spending habits! Create a spreadsheet with the headings shown below and enter your own values for a month. (Accuracy and honesty are not essential here!)

> Food
> Travel
> Books
> Stationery
> Clothes
> Entertainment
> Other
> Saving

1 Select the table of data, including the headings.

2 Click the **Chart Wizard** tool ![].

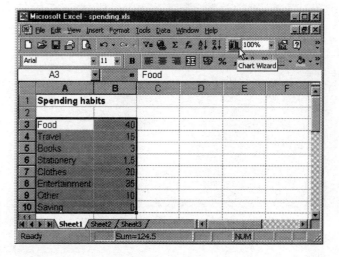

3 Select *Pie* as the **Chart Type,** and a simple pie or a whole pie with 3-D effect as the **sub-type** then click **Next.**

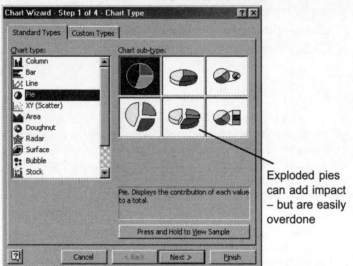

Exploded pies can add impact – but are easily overdone

4 At Step 2, check the **Series in** setting – the spending habits figures are in *Columns.* Click **Next.**

5 At Step 3, on the **Legend** tab, turn off the legend display.

6 Switch to the **Data Labels** tab and select **Show label and percent** or **Show label.**

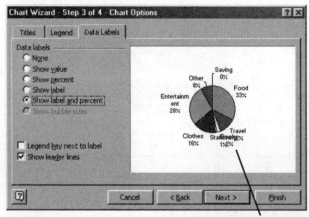

7 Click **Finish.**

The preview only a guide – the finshed chart will look better

If you have any small values, the pie slices will be thin and the data labels will overlap. You may need to adjust the relative sizes of the chart and the text.

1 Click on the chart just outside the pie to select the plot area.

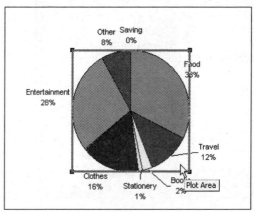

2 Drag a handle to increase the size of the whole pie.
3 Right-click on any data label, select **Format Data Labels...** and set the font size to suit the chart.

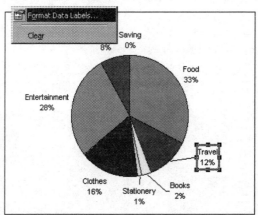

4 If a label overlaps another, click on it to select it, then drag it to where there is more space.

7.6 Saving and printing

Saving

Charts are saved as part of the Excel workbook or Word or PowerPoint document in which they are created, so you do not have to do a special save routine. But – as always – you should save your file regularly and whenever you have made any significant additions or changes to it.

Printing

Charts inserted into Word or PowerPoint documents are printed as part of the document. In Excel you can print a chart by itself, or as part of the sheet in which it is placed. If you want to print it as

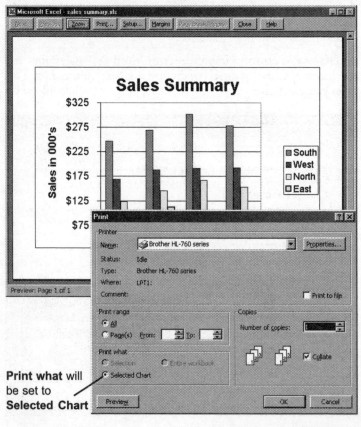

Print what will be set to **Selected Chart**

part of a sheet, make sure that it is included in the Print Area then print as normal (see page 117).

To print a chart by itself:

1 Click anywhere in the chart.
2 From the **File** menu select **Print Preview**.
3 Check the appearance then click **Print...**
4 Set the options as required and click **OK**.

7.7 Microsoft Graph

Microsoft Graph is an Office accessory – it can only be used within another program such as Word, and not separately. Its facilities are almost identical to those in Excel. The tools and options are the same, and you have the same range of types and sub-types. In fact, the only real difference is the source of the data – Microsoft Graph has its own little datasheet.

To create a Microsoft Graph object in Word or PowerPoint, use the **Insert > Chart** or **Insert > Picture > Chart** commands. This gives you a datasheet with dummy data, and a bar chart based on

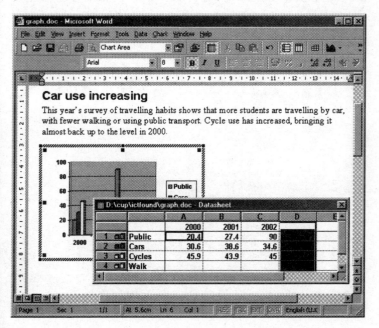

it. If you want a bar chart, just replace the dummy data with your own, but the chart type can easily by changed if you like.

1 Click into the document where you want to place the chart.

2 Open the **Insert** menu, point to **Picture** and select **Chart**.

3 Replace the dummy data with your own, deleting any unwanted cells.

4 If you want to change the type, open the **Chart** menu and select **Chart Type...**

5 Use the Formatting toolbar and the Chart menu options to format the chart.

6 Click into the document when you have finished creating and formatting the chart.

7 Click once on the chart to select it, then drag a handle to resize.

8 Double-click on the chart if you need to edit the data or change the formatting.

Chart position

Like any inserted object, a chart will be placed at the current cursor position, left-aligned and 'in line' with the text – i.e. the text will stop on the line above it and start again below the chart.

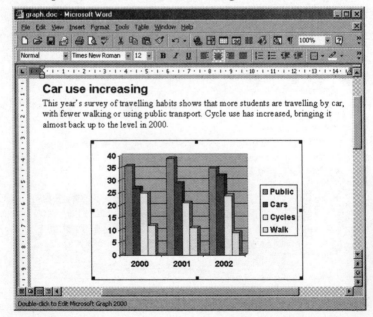

To change the chart's alignment:

• Select the chart and click the left, centre or right alignment button.

To change how the chart relates to the text:

• Right-click on the chart and select **Format Object...** At the dialog box, go to the **Layout** tab and select a **Wrapping style**.

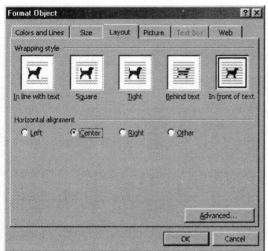

Whatever the wrapping style, the chart can be dragged to anywhere on a page

7.8 Exercise

This exercise builds on the spending habits worksheet from the section on pie charts (page 177).

1 Open the spending habits worksheet. Add suitable figures for two more months, and type the month names into the tops of the columns.

2 Select the data with its row and column headers (A2 to D10, if you use the layout shown in the screenshot on page 184).

3 Click the **Chart Wizard** button.

4 Work through the Wizard to produce a bar (column) chart.

5 Make sure that the series are in *rows* – the month names should be used for the X axis, and the types of spending for the labels in the legend.

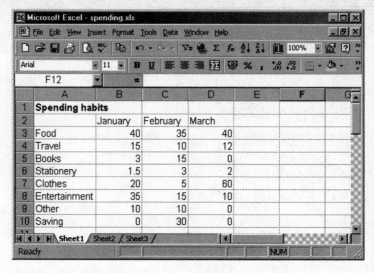

6 Add the chart title 'Spending habits'.
7 The chart should be created on a new sheet.
8 Print the chart to file.
9 Save the file as *spending2.xls*.

Summary

+ There are different types of charts. The most commonly used types are bar charts, line graphs and pie charts.

+ Charts and graphs can be produced easily with the Chart Wizard in Excel.

+ Labels on the axes and the legend help to clarify the meaning of a chart.

+ A chart can be printed separately from the rest of a sheet – just select it, then start the Print routine.

+ If you want to create a chart in a Word or PowerPoint document, insert a Microsoft Graph object.

08

computer art

In this chapter you will learn

- about types of graphics software
- how to use Paint
- about the Drawing tools
- how to manipulate drawn objects
- how to format images

8.1 Computer graphics

There are many graphics applications currently in use. They can be divided into two main categories according to the way images are created and stored: *bitmap* and *vector*.

In bitmap graphics software, the screen is treated like an artist's canvas. When a line, shape or dot of colour is applied, it becomes part of the whole picture. You may be able to undo the last few changes, but you cannot select a line, shape or dot and move it, resize or edit it. The picture is stored by recording the colour of each pixel (bit) of the screen (the map). The Windows accessory, Paint is an example of a simple bitmap graphics application.

With vector graphics, the image is defined by the size, angle, colour and other properties of the lines and shapes that make it up. These remain separate elements, and can be selected and edited at any time. Microsoft Draw is an example of a simple vector graphics application. Draw is not a separate program, but an accessory supplied with the Microsoft Office suite.

8.2 Paint

I use Paint regularly – it's ideal for trimming and tidying screenshots for books, though I don't expect many of you will want it for this purpose. Though it can be used to produce intricate images, these require a great deal of time and skill – and can be created more successfully on a computer art package, with a full set of shading, shaping and manipulating tools. Paint is probably best used to draw simple diagrams, or as a children's toy, or to get an idea of how this type of graphics software works.

Screenshots

If you press the [**Prt Sc**] (Print Screen) key, the whole screen display will be copied into the Clipboard. If you press [**Alt**] + [**Prt Sc**] then only the active window will be copied into the Clipboard. The image can then be pasted into Paint, or any other graphics program, and saved from there. That's how the screenshots were produced for this book.

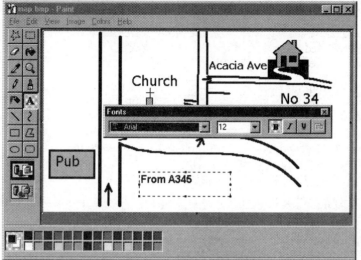

Figure 8.1 Using Paint to create a diagram. The **Text toolbar** gives you the full range of fonts and the main style effects.

The Toolbox

There is a simple but adequate set of tools. A little experimentation will show how they all work.

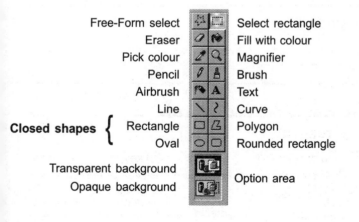

Free-Form select	Select rectangle
Eraser	Fill with colour
Pick colour	Magnifier
Pencil	Brush
Airbrush	Text
Line	Curve
Closed shapes { Rectangle	Polygon
Oval	Rounded rectangle
Transparent background	
Opaque background	Option area

Most of them have options that can be set in the area below the toolbar.

- When you select an area (or paste an image from file or from the Clipboard) the background can be transparent or opaque.
- You can set the size of the Eraser, Brush, Airbrush, Line and Curve. N.B. the Line thickness applies to the closed shapes.
- The Magnifier is 4× by default, but can be 2×, 6× or 8×.
- The Pencil is only ever 1 pixel wide.
- Closed shapes can be outline or fill only, or both.

The Curve is probably the trickiest of the tools to use. The line can have one or two curves to it.

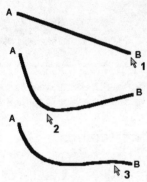

1   Draw a line between the points where the curve will start and end.

2   Drag on the line to create the first curve – exaggerate the curve as it will be reduced at the next stage.

3   If the line is to have a second curve, drag it out now – as long as the mouse button is down, the line will flex to follow the cursor.

4   For a simple curve, just click at the end of the line.

Undo it!

If you go wrong any time – and you will with the Curve – use **Edit > Undo**. This removes the effect of the last action.

Working with selected areas

The rectangular and free-form selectors can be used to select an area of the screen. Once selected, an area can be:

- Deleted – use this for removing mistakes and excess bits.
- Copied – handy for creating repeating patterns.
- Saved as a file – use **Edit > Copy To...** and give a filename.
- Dragged elsewhere on screen.

- Flipped (mirrored) horizontally or vertically, or rotated in 90° increments – use **Image > Flip/Rotate** for these effects.
- Stretched – to enlarge, shrink or distort, or skew, either horizontally or vertically – use **Image > Stretch/Skew**.

Colours

The colour palette is used in almost the same way in all Windows programs. You can select a colour from the basic set – use the left button for the foreground colour and the right button for the background – or you can mix your own colours.

Double-click on a colour in the **Color Box** or use **Colors > Edit Colors** to open the **Edit Colors** panel. Initially only the **Basic colors** will be visible. Click **Define Custom Colors** to open the full panel.

To define a new colour, drag the cross-hair cursor in the main square to set the Red/Green/Blue balance, and move the arrow up or down the left scale to set the light/dark level. Colours can also be set by typing in values, but note that you are mixing light, not paint. Red and green make yellow; red, green and blue make grey/ white; the more you use, the lighter the colour.

When you have the colour you want, click **Add to Custom Colors**. The new colour will replace the one currently selected in the Color Box on the main screen.

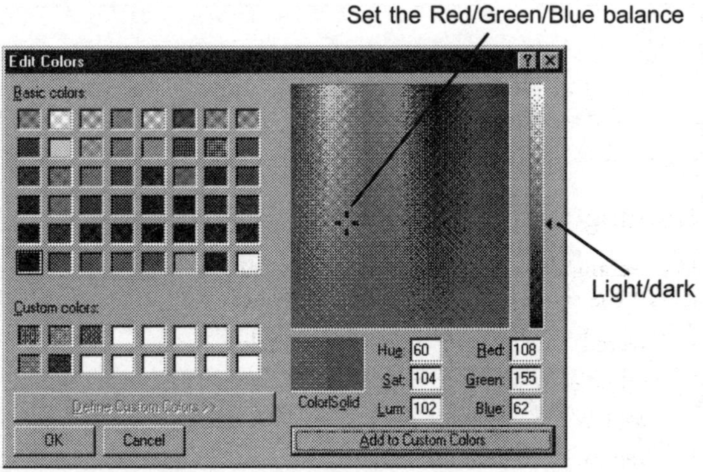

Figure 8.2 Editing colours in Paint.

Filing

Saving and opening files is the same here as in Word. You can also use **Edit > Copy To...** to save a selected area of an image and **Edit > Paste From...** to open a file so that you can combine it with the existing picture. The image will come in as a selected area, which can be positioned wherever required. Set the background to transparent to merge the two images, or to opaque for the new file to overlay the old image.

8.3 Microsoft Draw

Draw is not so much a separate program, as a set of drawing tools that can be called up in any Microsoft Office application.

It can be used in two separate ways:

◆ Elements can be drawn, as separate items, in amongst the ordinary text.

◆ You can create a Draw object within a document. If the object is moved or resized, all the drawn elements inside it are moved and resized along with it.

To draw single elements, perhaps to add a line or arrow to some text, you only need to have the Drawing toolbar visible.

To display the drawing toolbar:

1 Right-click on any toolbar to display the list of toolbars.

2 Click **Drawing** so that a tick appears on its left.

For the rest of this chapter, we will be working in Draw objects. The drawing techniques are the same in both approaches.

8.4 Starting a drawing

When you start a new drawing, a 'canvas' is marked out on the screen and the AutoShapes toolbar appears. The canvas can be resized at any time, and moved into place once you have finished.

1 Click into the document where you want the drawing to go.

2 Open the **Insert** menu, point to **Picture** and select **New Drawing**. Wait a moment.

The Draw toolbar

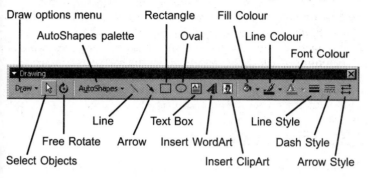

To draw simple rectangles or ovals:

3 Click on the tool.

4 Click where you want one corner of the shape to be placed.

5 Drag to create the shape.

• To produce a perfect square (or circle), hold down [**Shift**] while you draw a rectangle (or oval).

Click where you want the drawing

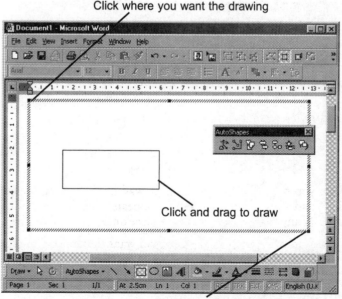

Click and drag to draw

Drag a handle to adjust the size

To return to the document:

6 Click anywhere on the document outside the drawing.

To edit the drawing again later:

7 Double-click inside the drawing.

8.5 Lines and arrows

Lines and arrows are drawn and formatted in the same way, and are interchangeable – an arrow is a line with a head on the end.

To draw a line or arrow:

1 Click on the tool.

2 Click where you want one end of the line.

3 Drag to the required length.

To adjust a line or arrow:

4 Click on the line to select it.

5 Drag on the middle of the line to move it.

6 Drag on a handle to change the angle or length.

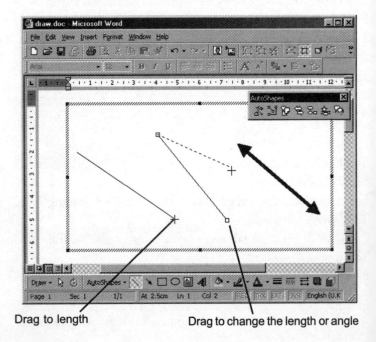

Drag to length

Drag to change the length or angle

To format a line or arrow:

7 Select the line then pick from the options on the drop-down lists from the Line Style, Dash Style and Arrow Style tools.

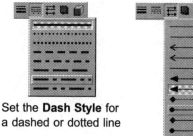

Set the **Dash Style** for a dashed or dotted line

More Arrows...

The **Line Style** sets the thickness

Use the **Arrow Style** options, to point to objects or link them

8.6 Filled shapes

Any closed shape can be filled with solid or shaded colour, or a pattern or texture.

1 Select the shape.

2 Click on the **Fill Color** button.

To fill with solid colour:

3 Click on a colour.

4 If the colour you want is not in the palette, click **More Fill Colors...** and select from the full range in the **Colors** dialog box.

To fill with shaded colour:

5 Click **Fill Effects**.

6 On the **Gradient** tab, select the **Color**(s) and the **Shading Style**.

To fill with a texture:

7 Go to the **Texture** tab and select a texture from the list.

To fill with a pattern:

8 On the **Pattern** tab, select the **Pattern**, then the **Foreground** and **Background** colours.

9 Click **OK**.

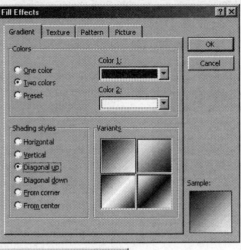

Gradients can be based on one colour and white, or two colours, and the shading can flow in any direction – keep an eye on the sample while you explore the variations

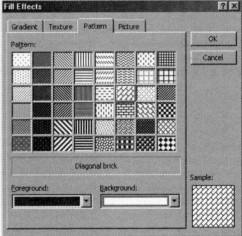

You can also fill a shape with a picture – select and insert one from the **Picture** tab

With 48 patterns in any foreground and background colours, you can create an almost infinite range of fill effects

Copying objects

To copy a drawn object, select it and use **Edit > Copy**, or click the **Copy** button ![copy], then use **Edit > Paste** or click the **Paste** button ![paste] to create a copy of the object. It will appear close to the original object – drag it into position.

8.7 Rotate and flip

The menu that opens from the Draw button holds options for manipulating objects, including these Rotate and Flip commands:

* **Free Rotate** – allows you to rotate the object by any amount around its centre
* **Rotate Left** – rotates it 90° anticlockwise
* **Rotate Right** – rotates it 90° clockwise
* **Flip Horizontal** – reflects it as if it were next to a mirror
* **Flip Vertical** – reflects it as if it were on top of a mirror.

Most of these work by first selecting the object then giving the command. **Free Rotate** is different.

To use Free Rotate:

1 Click **Draw**, point to **Rotate or Flip** and select **Free Rotate**.

Or

2 Select the **Free Rotate** tool.

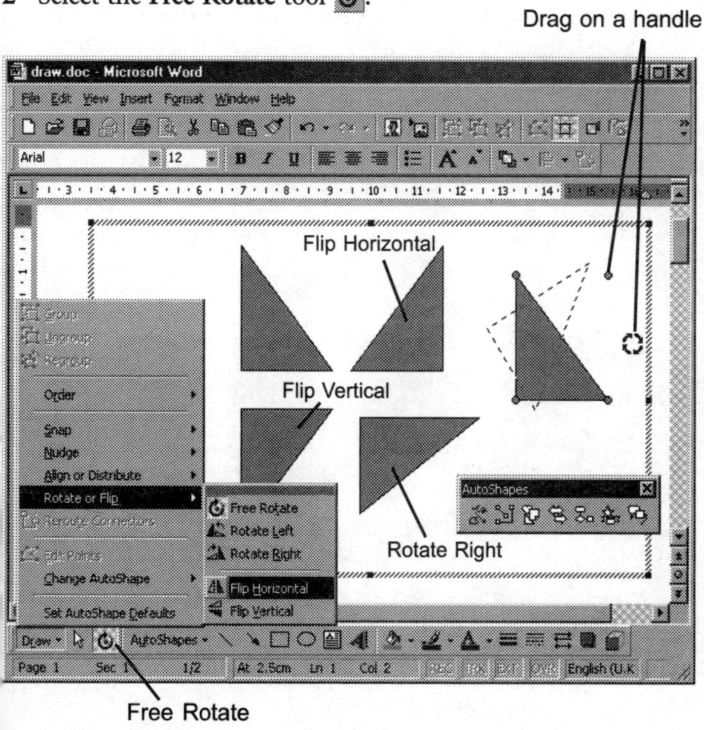

Drag on a handle

Free Rotate

3 Click on the object – the green rotate handles will appear.

4 Drag on one of the green handles to pull the object round – a dotted outline will show you how it will look.

5 Click on the background to turn off the rotate handles.

8.8 Text in drawings

Drawn objects can be placed directly amongst text, but this is not the best way to combine text and drawings.

With a text box, you can place your text exactly where you want it in the drawing.

1 Select the **Text Box** tool 🖺.

2 Click at one corner of where you want to draw the box, and drag to the opposite corner.

3 Type your text.

4 Select the text and format it as usual, with the tools on the **Formatting** toolbar and the options on the **Format** menu.

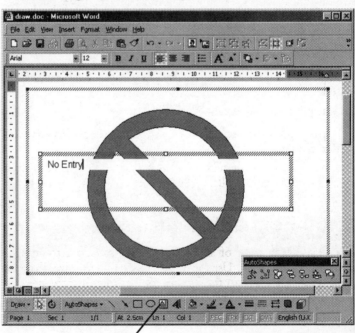

Text box tool

5 If you want to move or resize the text box, click on an edge to select the box rather than its text, then drag on a frame or handle to move or resize the object. Note that enlarging the box does not enlarge the text – if you want to change the text size use the **Font size** option in the Formatting toolbar.

You have the same range of formatting options here as with any other text – remember to select it first.

8.9 Importing images

We saw in Section 6.10 how to import images from file or the Clip Gallery into a publication. They can be imported into a Drawing or directly into a Word document in much the same way.

To import a picture into a drawing:

1 Open the **Insert** menu and select **Clip Art...** or **Picture from File...**

To import a picture into a Word document:

1 Open the **Insert** menu and select **Picture** then **Clip Art...** or **From File...**

2 The picture can then be selected from the files on your disks or from the Clip Gallery. See Section 6.10.

8.10 Formatting images

The final appearance of any picture – file or clip art – can be adjusted at any point. Use the mouse to change the size, shape or position or the tools on the **Picture** toolbar to adjust the colours, crop it or set how the text wraps around it.

1 Select the picture.

2 Drag a handle to adjust the size.

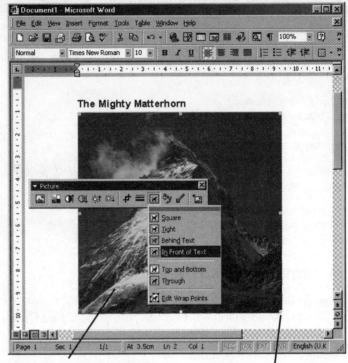

Drag on the image to move it   Drag on a handle to resize

3 Drag anywhere within the area to move.

4 Use the **Picture** tools to adjust the settings.

The Picture toolbar

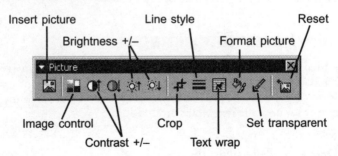

Insert picture lets you replace the picture with another from file.

The **Image control** options set the basic colours:

    Automatic – in its normal colours;

    Grayscale – for output to black-only printers;

    Black & White – for high-contrast printing, use with line drawings or for special effects;

    Watermark – ultra-pale, for use as background.

Contrast +/– and **Brightness +/–** do what you would expect.

Line style sets the thickness of lines in drawn objects.

Crop turns the Crop tool on. Drag on a side or corner handle to cut unwanted material off the sides of a picture.

Text wrap controls how the picture sits in relation to text on the page. Most of the options here are the same as those on the **Layout** tab of the **Format Picture** dialog box. The **Edit Wrap Points** option allows you to mould text around an irregular shape – click anywhere on the outline to create a point, then drag it in or out to adjust the outline.

Format Picture opens the **Format Picture** dialog box. This gives you more accurate control of the size, position and layout.

When you resize a picture, lock the aspect ratio to keep it in the same proportion

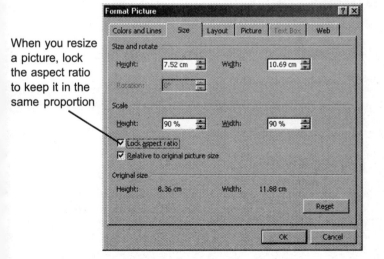

Set transparent will make a selected colour transparent, so that the document background – and anything that is written on it – will show through. To use it, click on the tool, then click on any area of the colour.

Reset restores the image to how it was before you messed it up!

Resizing images

If you enlarge or shrink a bitmapped image, smooth curves tend to become jagged. This is because the images are composed of dots. When enlarged the dots become blocks and when reduced some dots are removed. The coarsening effect is particularly noticeable on small circles and text. In vector graphic images, the lines, shapes and characters are scaled up from patterns using mathematical formulae, and redrawn when they are resized. The result is that lines and curves have smooth edges at any size.

The effect is also noticeable in printed output. Modern printers have a resolution of 600 or more dots per inch. A 15" monitor set to display 800×640 has a resolution of around 70 dots per inch. An 800×640 bitmapped picture will look 'dotty' when it is printed if it is more than 2" wide.

8.11 Save and print

Drawn objects are part of the documents in which they are drawn. They are saved when the document is saved, and are printed as part of the normal document printing routine. If you only want to print a drawing, either create it in a new document, or put it on a page by itself and at the **Print** dialog box select that page number in the Print range.

8.12 Exercise

Use the drawing tools to create an image that could be used as an inlay for a CD case. The image should be 120mm square. It should contain at least one example of text, drawn object and imported file or clip art image.

Summary

- A bitmap image is created by colouring the pixels, much as pictures are created on paper with paints or inks. Windows Paint is a bitmap graphics program.

- Vector images are composed of individual elements that can be selected and edited at any time. Microsoft Draw is a vector graphics program.

- The Draw tools can be used to create single lines or shapes in a document.

- You can draw lines, arrows, rectangles, ovals and autoshapes. Closed shapes can be filled with shaded or solid colour, patterns or textures.

- Drawn objects can be resized, rotated and flipped.

- Images can be imported into a drawing or directly into a document. Imported images can be formatted with the tools on the Picture toolbar.

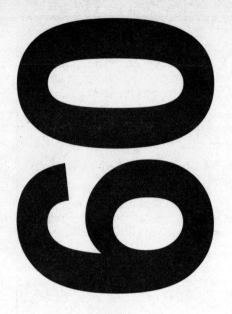

09

web pages

In this chapter you will learn

- how to create HTML files
- how HTML tags work
- how to format text and add images to a Web page
- how to create links between pages

9.1 HTML and Web pages

HTML – HyperText Markup Language – is the system used to produce Web pages. It is a set of tags (codes) that format text, draw lines, display images and handle links to other pages. HTML is not difficult to learn or to use. You need no special equipment. The page files can be created on any text editor or word processor that can save files as plain text – Notepad is just as good as Word for HTML. And, of course, the pages can be viewed and tested on any browser – the prime purpose of a browser is to display Web pages, which are HTML files.

HTML editors and saving in HTML format

An HTML editor is an application which gives you a WYSIWYG (What You See Is What You Get) display in which to create Web pages. Formatting text and inserting images is done in much the same way in these as in Word. There are many commercial and free editors around, including FrontPage Express, which is supplied with Internet Explorer. (Look in the **Start > Programs > Internet Tools** menu to see if it is installed on your PC.)

Word, and most other modern word processors and DTP applications, can also save documents in HTML format, so that you can create your Web pages using familiar tools.

It is certainly quicker and easier to produce Web pages with a WYSIWYG application, but there are disadvantages. These applications cannot usually handle some of the more advanced aspects of HTML; and they all produce clumsy code. An HTML file created in an editor or output from Word will be anything up to twice as large as one produced 'by hand'. They tend to duplicate formatting instructions and typically carry a lot of information about when, how and by whom the page was created.

However you are going to create your Web pages in future, you should at least understand the basics of HTML – if nothing else, you need to for the CLAIT assessment!

View the source code

The **View > Source** command will show you the HTML code behind any Web page that you open in your browser.

9.2 Tags

There are only a limited number of tags and they all follow fairly strict rules.

All tags are enclosed in <angle brackets> and they are normally used in pairs – one at the start and one at the end of the text that they affect. For example:

```
<H1> This is a main heading </H1>
```

Notice that the closing tag is almost the same as the opening tag. The only difference is that it has a forward slash at the start.

You can have tags inside other tags, but they must be 'nested' properly. We'll come back to this in a moment.

A few tags are used singly. For example:

```
<BR>
```

This creates a 'BReak' – forcing the following text to start on a new line.

Tags can be written in lower or upper case.

```
<BR>  <Br>      <br>
```

These all have exactly the same effect.

9.3 Web pages

All pages have the same outline structure. Here is a simple page. The indenting helps to show the structure, but is not essential.

```
<HTML>
   <HEAD>
      <TITLE>My Home Page</TITLE>
   </HEAD>
   <BODY>
      Welcome to my Web
   </BODY>
</HTML>
```

The whole text is enclosed by the tags <HTML> and </HTML>

The <HEAD> area holds information about the page. Anything written here is not displayed in the browser, except the <TITLE>

which is the text that will appear in the browser's Title bar when the page is loaded. This can be left blank.

The <BODY> area is where the main code goes.

• Notice how the tags are 'nested'. The <TITLE> pair are inside the <HEAD> pair, which are inside the <HMTL> pair.

To create your first Web page:

1 Type your HTML text into a text editor or word processor – use the simple example on page 204.

2 Save the document as plain text, with an *.htm* extension, e.g. *mypage.htm*

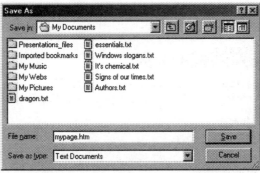

3 Start your browser – don't go online – and use **File > Open** to load in the document.

4   Look at the result and compare it with your text file.

The <TITLE> text appears here

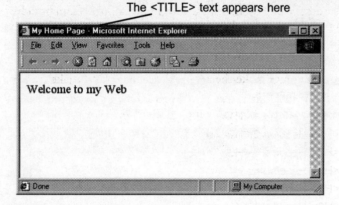

9.4   Formatting text

Any untagged text written in the BODY area will be displayed in the browser in the standard font (usually Times New Roman, size 12 point) and in a continuous block – no matter how neatly you formatted it and laid it out in your HTML file.

If you want to vary the size and style of text, or to break it into separate paragraphs, you must use the text formatting tags.

Paragraphs and breaks

Create separate paragraphs with these tags:

   <P> </P>

Start a new paragaph with a space before and after. The closing tag </P> can be omitted.

Start the following text on a new line, but without creating a space between the two.

When a browser reads an HTML document, it ignores all spaces (apart from a single space between words), tabs and new lines. What this means is that it doesn't matter how you lay out your HTML text. You can indent it, and add line breaks if you like, to make it easier for you to read, but these will not change what your readers see. Only the tags affect the layout of the page in the browser.

Headings

There are six levels of headings, with a range of sizes from (roughly) 24 point down to 9 point. The sizes relative to other headings and to plain text are constant, though the actual sizes depend upon the Text Size setting in the browser.

All heading tags make the enclosed text bold, and make it into a separate paragraph.

```
<H1> Heading 1</H1>
<H2> Heading 2</H2>
<H3> Heading 3</H3>
<H4> Heading 4</H4>
<H5> Heading 5</H5>
<H6> Heading 6</H6>
```

Emphasis

If you want to emphasize some text, you can make it bold or italic with these tags:

```
<B> Bold </B>
<I> Italic </I>
```

You can use the tags within paragraphs to pick out single words or phrases, or you can enclose any number of paragraphs in one pair to apply the effect to the whole set.

1 Type this HTML code into your editor, save it as headings.htm and view it in a browser.

```
<HTML>
   <HEAD>
      <TITLE>Headings</TITLE>
   </HEAD>
   <BODY>
   <H1>This is Heading 1</H1>
   <H2>This is Heading 2</H2>
   <H3>This is Heading 3</H3>
   <H4>This is Heading 4</H4>
   From H5 down, the headings are smaller than normal text
   <H5>This is Heading 5</H5>
   <H6>This is Heading 6</H6>
   <P>Normal text looks like this. </P>
```

```
        <P>The P tags produce <B>a line space </B>between
        paragraphs</P>
        If you use a Break tag, <BR>
        the following text appears on a new line, but
        <I>immediately </I>below
    </BODY>
</HTML>
```

2 Note the relative differences between the sizes of the headings.

3 Open the **View** menu, point to **Text Size** and select a larger or
   smaller size, and see how it affects the display.

Figure 9.1 The heading tags set the relative size of lines of text,
but the actual size depends upon the browser that it is viewed in.

Alignment

Body text and headings are normally aligned to the left edge, but
both can be set in the centre or to the right, if required.

To set the alignment, you write inside the <H ...> or <P> tag the
keyword ALIGN = followed by *Center*, *Right* or *Left*. (Left is never
needed – a simple <P> will left align text – but it can sometimes

help to make the coding easier to read.) When text is used as an option value, as here, it can be enclosed in double quotes. This is only essential when the text consists of two or more words.

For example:

```
<H2 ALIGN = "Right">
```

starts a right-aligned heading. </H2> closes it.

```
<P ALIGN = "Center">
```

makes the following paragraph align to the centre of the window.

Note that the US spelling CENTER must be used in the tags.

This example demonstrates the ALIGN clause in action.

```
<HTML>
   <BODY>
      <H1 ALIGN = "Center"> Text Alignment</H1>
      <P ALIGN = "Center"> Set in the centre of the window
      <BR>
      As many lines as you like from one ALIGN
      <P>Back to normal
      <P ALIGN = "Right"> Align to the right
      <P ALIGN = "Left"> Align to the left. This is the same as
      not setting an ALIGN option. Note that long lines wrap round
      to fit the window size.
   </BODY>
</HTML>
```

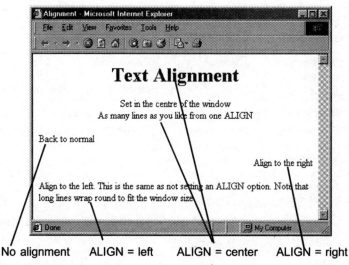

No alignment   ALIGN = left   ALIGN = center   ALIGN = right

9.5 Colours

Text-only pages are fast to load, but can be a bit boring. Colour adds impact to your pages, without adding to the loading time.

BODY colours

The colours of the background and text of the page can be set by the BGCOLOR and TEXT options in the BODY tag.

```
<BODY BGCOLOR = value TEXT = value>
```

FONT COLOR

At any point on the page, you can change the colour of the text with the tag:

```
<FONT COLOR = value >
```

The colour is used for all following text until it is reset with another <FONT COLOR = ... > tag or you use a closing </FONT> tag to revert to the standard body text colour.

Colour values

Colours can be specified in two ways. It is possible to define a colour by specifying the proportion of red, green and blue to use. Far simpler, you can identify 16 basic colours using standard names – these should be enough for most purposes.

Black	Red	Lime	Blue
Yellow	Fuchsia	Aqua	White
Maroon	Green	Navy	Purple
Olive	Teal	Gray *	Silver

* Note the US spelling

The colour names can be enclosed in double quotes to make them stand out, but this is not essential. Like all HTML keywords, they are not case-sensitive. Some examples of colour settings:

```
<BODY BGCOLOR = "Maroon">
```

sets the background to dark red.

```
<BODY TEXT = blue>
```

sets the text colour to bright blue.

```
<BODY BGCOLOR = Black TEXT = Yellow>
```

sets the background to black and the text to yellow.

```
<FONT COLOR = "Gray"> Donkey </FONT>
```

sets 'Donkey' in grey, then reverts to the previous colour.

Use code shown below to test out the range of colours. Try it with the values given here, then experiment with other hexadecimal values and the colour names.

```
<HTML>
   <HEAD>
      <TITLE>Colour test</TITLE>
   </HEAD>
   <BODY BGCOLOR = White TEXT = Black>
      <H1>Colour test</H1>
      Let's get bright and cheerful
      <BR><FONT COLOR = "Red"> Red
      <BR><FONT COLOR = "Green"> Green
      <BR><FONT COLOR = "Blue"> Blue
      <BR></FONT>Back to green, </FONT> then to red,
      </FONT> then to black
   </BODY>
</HTML>
```

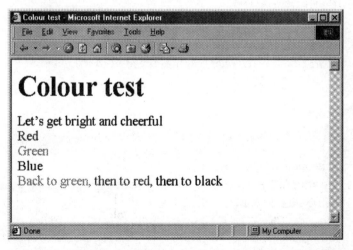

Figure 9.2 Notice how the </FONT> tags turn off the latest colour setting, making the earlier setting active. Compare the screen with the code: </FONT>Back to green, </FONT> then to red, </FONT> then to black.

9.6   Using images

Images can add a great deal to the appearance of a page, but at a cost. Image files are large compared with text files and will increase download time. A screenful of text is around 1Kb – almost instant downloading – but a screen-sized picture could be anything up to 300Kb and take nearly 2 minutes to come in. So, include images, but keep visitors happy by following these rules:

*   Keep the images as small as possible;
*   If you want to display large images, e.g. your photo gallery, put them on separate pages and tell visitors how big they are.
*   Include text describing the image, for the benefit of those who browse with image-loading turned off.

The basic image tag is:

    <IMG SRC = "filename">

The quotes around the filename are only essential if there are spaces in it.

The <IMG> tag has several options. The ALT option is important and should be used:

    ALT = "description"

This is the text that is displayed if you hold the mouse pointer over the image. It is also what will be displayed if the image is not loaded into a browser. In the example opposite, if image loading was turned off, you would see this instead of the top picture:

Montsegur in Languedoc

File formats

Images for Web pages should be GIF or JPEG files. These are the only formats that all browsers can cope with (Internet Explorer can also display BMP images).

*   GIF images are limited to 256 colours, which is fine for cartoons and drawings.
*   JPG images can have up to 16 million colours, which makes them suitable for photographs and other complex images, but they are saved in a compressed format, producing small files.

Both formats are very economical. In the example opposite, the mountain image is 33Kb as a JPG file, but 420Kb as a BMP; the mouse is 3.2Kb as a GIF but 27Kb as a BMP.

Taking this code as a pattern, but using your own pictures, create a Web page with one or more images. Give each image suitable ALT text.

```
<HTML>
  <HEAD>
    <TITLE>Images</TITLE>
  </HEAD>
  <BODY>
    <H1>Images on Web pages</H1>
    <IMG SRC = mountain.jpg ALT = "Montsegur in Languedoc"  >
    <P>JPEG images can have up to 16 million colours. Use this
```

Figure 9.3 The ALT text shows when you pause over an image.

format (with .JPG or .JPEG extension) for photos, like this.</P>
<IMG SRC = mouse.gif ALT = "Mouse with a mouse" >
GIFs can only have 256 colours, but take little space. Use them
for cartoon and drawings.
  </BODY>
</HTML>

9.7   Hyperlinks

Hyperlinks are the basis of the World Wide Web. They allow browsers to move easily from one page to another within a site and between sites throughout the linked Web. They can also be used to link to other parts of the Internet.

A link is created with a pair of tags. The first contains the URL of the page or file to be linked, and takes the form:

    <A HREF=URL> text or image </A>

You can create links to:

+ another part of the same page
+ another page on the same site
+ to a page anywhere else on the Web
+ to any file on the Internet
+ to an e-mail address.

We are only interested in the first three kinds of links here.

Links to other pages

Most Web sites consist of a number of pages all linked together. A simple site for a small firm might have these four pages:

index.htm	Hello and welcome
products.htm	What we sell
services.htm	We also do this
contacts.htm	Address, phone and e-mail

Visitors to the site normally arrive at the home page – which is usually called *index.htm* or *index.html*. They then need to be able to get from there to the products and services pages, and to move from any page to the contacts page so that they can place an order.

To link to another page on the same site – and stored in the same folder – you need only give its filename.

For example:

```
<A HREF = contacts.htm>Contact us</A>
```

This will be displayed as <u>Contact us</u> and clicking on the text will load in the contacts page.

Links to other sites

To link to another site, you give its URL in just the same way as in a browser. If you are linking to the home page, then only the site name is needed, e.g.

```
<A HREF=www.yahoo.com>Go to Yahoo!</A>
```

If you want to link to a page within the site, then you need the site name and the page name. You will probably also need to include the path down to the folders in which the page file is stored. For example, the 'home page' for HTML at W3 – the organization that defined HTML – is called *MarkUp.html* and is in the *MarkUp* folder. This will create a link to it:

```
<A HREF = www.w3.org/MarkUp/MarkUp.html> Click here to
go to the HTML home page </A>
```

Links within the page

If you have a page that runs over several screens, including links within the page will let your readers jump from one part to another. The clickable link follows the same pattern as above, but you must first define a named place, or *anchor*, to jump to.

```
<A NAME = Top> Start here</A>
```

The anchor tags can be placed around any text or image. They do not do anything except identify the place and nothing shows on screen.

The HREF tag sets the anchor as the target, but with a hash (#) before the anchor name. This is essential.

```
<A HREF = #Top> Return to top of page </A>
```

Links on images

To make an image into a link, write the IMG tag inside the HREF:

```
<A HREF = contacts.htm> <IMG SRC = letter.gif ALT = Contact
page> </A>
```

Linked images are normally displayed with a blue outline, to match the blue underline of text links.

```
<HTML>
<HEAD>
   <TITLE>Links</TITLE>
</HEAD>
<BODY>
   <A NAME = Top><H1>Welcome to my World</H1></A>
   This page will tell you all you want to know about me, and more!
   <P>I run a train-spotting club. You can reach it <A HREF =
   trainclub.htm>here</A>
   <P>Visit my friend Bob <A HREF = www.bobsplace.co.fr>
```

Figure 9.4   The two internal links in this page – down to the cat and back to the top – are both visible in this example, but you only need links in pages that are too big to fit in a normal browser window.

```
<IMG SRC = bob.gif></A>
<P>Meet my cat, <A HREF = #tiddles>Tiddles.</A>
<P>Contact me <A HREF = contacts.htm><IMG SRC = letter.gif
ALT = Contacts page></A>
<P>
<A NAME = tiddles><H3>Tiddles</H3></A>
<P>This is my cat. Isn't she a beauty!
<IMG SRC = mycat.jpg ALT = Tiddles>
<BR>
<A HREF = #Top>Back to top</A>
</BODY>
</HTML>
```

9.8 Printing HTML files

An HTML file can be printed in two forms:

*   As the source code text from within the text editor or word processor. See page 42 (NotePad) or page 66 (Word).

*   As a Web page, by loading it into a browser and using its Print routine (see page 98).

9.9 Exercise

1   Plan, and sketch on paper, a set of three linked pages to make a simple site for a sports club. There should be a welcome page, with basic information about the club, a page to list events and activities, a page to give membership and contact details.

2   Create the HTML files for the three pages.

3   Load the welcome page and check that the links between it and the other two pages work properly.

4   Print the pages from the browser, then print the source code files from your word processor or text editor.

Summary

♦ You can create HTML files with specialized HTML editors, word processors or simple text editors.

♦ All HTML formatting is done using tags. These normally enclose the text or object to be formatted.

♦ You can easily set the size, alignment or colour of text, or make text bold or italic.

♦ Images for Web pages should be in GIF or JPG format.

♦ Hyperlinks enable you to jump within a page, or from one page to another in the same site or to a page anywhere in the World Wide Web.

♦ HTML files can be printed as source code text or as displayed Web pages.

presentation graphics

In this chapter you will learn

- about PowerPoint and presentations
- how to create new slides
- how to format text and bulleted lists
- how to add images
- about master slides, colour schemes and templates
- how to print slides and notes
- how to run a slide show

10.1 What is a presentation?

A presentation is a series of 'slides' that can be viewed on a computer, as overhead projections, through the Web or even as a proper slide show. PowerPoint is the leading presentation software.

A slide may contain:

* **text** – typically in bullet points;
* **images** – clip art, photographs and drawings;
* **video and sound clips** – or a recorded commentary;
* **graphs, organization charts** and other inserted objects.

All of these can be formatted in the usual ways, and put on a coloured or picture background.

The slides can be simply displayed one after the other, but if you want more, you can have animated transitions between slides, build slide displays one line or image at a time, or let the audience find its own way through the set.

Each slide can be accompanied by *notes*, which can be printed for the presenter's use, or printed as part of *handouts* for the audience. The handouts can be anything from simple reminders, with the slides printed in miniature, 9 to a page, or full course notes – you can even use PowerPoint in the same way as you would use Word, to produce full pages of text and images.

10.2 The PowerPoint screen

At the top of the screen are the Menu bar, and the Standard and Formatting toolbars – all similar to those in Word. At the bottom of the screen is the Drawing toolbar. (Other toolbars can be opened from the **View > Toolbars** menu.)

The screen has three panes:

* The **Slide pane** is where you build up and display the slides – normally one at a time.
* The **Outline pane** shows only the text on slides. The text can be added to or edited, and new slides can be added from here.
* The **Notes pane** holds the (optional) notes that can be printed out to accompany the slides.

You can move between the slides in either the Slide or the Outline pane.

Standard toolbar

Outline pane Formatting toolbar **Slide pane**

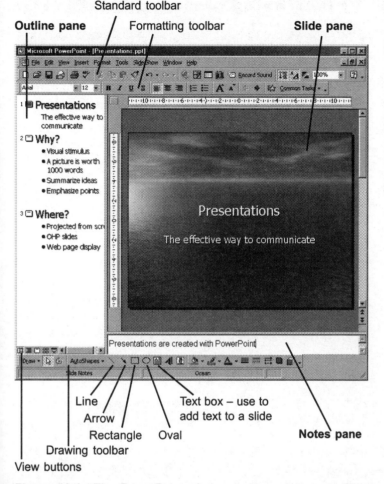

Line Text box – use to
Arrow add text to a slide
Rectangle Oval
Drawing toolbar **Notes pane**
View buttons

Figure 10.1 The PowerPoint window in Normal view. In Slide view the Slide pane takes up even more space; in Outline view, the Outline pane dominates the window.

Views

The PowerPoint display has six views.

- **Normal view** is best for general work. Here the Slide pane takes most of the space, with the Outline pane open to the left and the small Notes pane open below.

- In **Outline view** the Outline pane is dominant. Use this view when you want to concentrate on the text.

- In **Slide view** the Outline pane is reduced to a slim strip showing only the numbered symbols for the slides. Use this for working on the layout or for inserting objects.

- In **Slide Sorter view** the entire working area is used for thumbnails (small images) of the slides. This is a good view to use for rearranging the order.

- **Slide Show view** runs the presentation.

- **Notes Page** view shows the slide and its notes as it will appear when printed.

You can switch between the first five views by clicking the buttons at the bottom left of the status bar.

To get to Notes Page view, select **Notes Page** on the **View** menu.

10.3 Starting up

When you first start PowerPoint, you will be presented with the PowerPoint dialog box, from where you can start a new presentation or open an existing one.

Opening a presentation

At the PowerPoint dialog box:

1 Click **Open an existing presentation**.

2 Select from the list of recent presentations.

Or

3 Click **More Files...** and follow steps 5 to 7 below.

4 Click **OK**.

If you have a file open and want to open a second file...

5 From the **File** menu select **Open**.

6 Go to the right **Look in** folder.
7 Select a file – use the preview to identify the file.
8 Click **Open**.

The preview shows the first slide

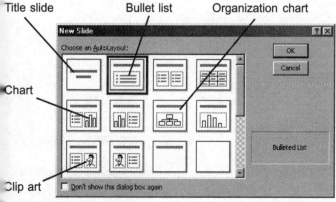

10.4 Creating slides

You can start with a completely blank slide, but it is simpler to begin with an AutoLayout from the **New Slide** dialog box. These have *placeholders* – formatted areas – for different types of text and objects.

1 The **New Slide** dialog box opens automatically when you start a presentation. To add slides later, use the 🔲 **New Slide** button.

Figure 10.2 The New Slide dialog box has a set of AutoLayouts.

2 Select an **AutoLayout** and click **OK**.

3 Replace the *Click to add text* prompts with your own text – just click on them and they disappear. Likewise, double-click in any object frame to add an object of that type.

10.5 Entering and editing text

Once you have text on a slide, it is edited and formatted exactly as in Word – the difference is in how you get the text there.

You cannot simply type onto a slide. Text can only be typed inside a text box. You can create one using the **Text box** tool on the Drawing toolbar, but it is simpler to start with a slide that contains a text placeholder.

The text box/placeholder can be moved and resized as required.

1 Click into the text box, delete the prompt and type your text.

2 Select the text.

3 Format it with the toolbar buttons and the font and size drop-down lists.

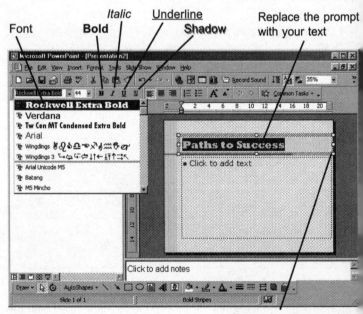

Font **Bold** *Italic* Underline Shadow — Replace the prompt with your text

Drag a handle to resize

4 Drag on the outline to move the box.

5 Drag on a handle to resize the box.

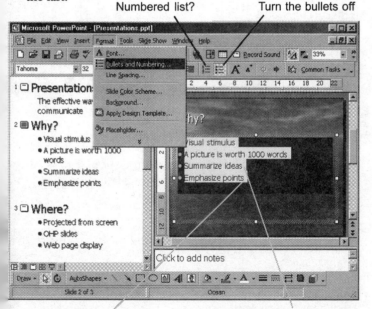

10.6 Bulleted lists

There are two types of text placeholders – titles (and subtitles)
and body text. Body text normally appears as bulleted lists, which
is usually what is required. The style, size and colour of the bullets
can be easily changed, and you can replace them with numbers or
turn them off completely.

To create a bulleted list:

1 Start from a slide with a bullets placeholder.

2 Click into the placeholder, type the text for the first point and
   press [**Enter**]. A bullet will be put in place for you at the start
   of the new line.

3 Repeat for the remaining points, but do not press [**Enter**] after
   the last.

Numbered list?   Turn the bullets off

No [Enter] at the end   [Enter] to start the next point

Figure 10.3   Creating a bulleted list – to format it, start with the
Format > Bullets and Numbering... command.

Formatting bulleted list:

1 Select the points, then…
2 To turn the bullets off, click the **Bullets** button ▤.
3 To replace them with numbers, click the **Numbering** button ▤.
4 To change the style, open the **Format** menu and select **Bullets and Numbering…**
5 Pick a bullet style and change the **Size** and **Color** as required.
6 Click **OK**.

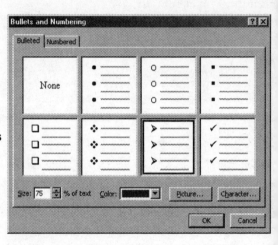

You can set the style, size and colour of bullets or of numbers

10.7   Images on slides

Images from files and clip art images are inserted in slightly different ways in PowerPoint. Clip art is the simplest to handle as you can start from a slide with a clip art object.

To create a slide with clip art:

1 Start from an AutoLayout containing a clip art object and double-click 🎨 .

Or

2 Use **Insert > Picture > Clip Art**.
3 Select a picture from the Gallery (see page 161 for Office 97 or page 162 for Office 2000).

4 To resize the picture, drag on one of the handles.

5 To format the picture, right-click on it and select **Show Picture Toolbar**. Use its tools to adjust the brightness, contrast, and other properties (see page 197).

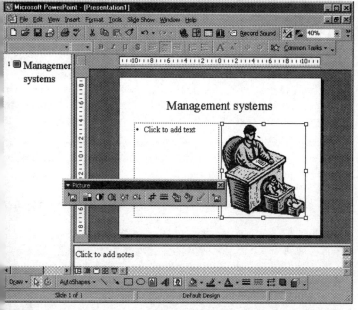

Figure 10.4 Clip art is quickly added if you start from a placeholder. Use the tools on the Picture toolbar to format it.

There are no AutoLayouts that are specially designed for images from file. You can start from one that has a non-specific 'Object' placeholder, but you then have to work through a slow, clunky insert object routine. It's simpler to start from a blank slide.

PowerPoint has built-in routines to display files in any of these formats: GIF, JPG, BMP, WMF (Windows metafile), EMF (enhanced metafile), PNG (portable network graphics). Other formats can be handled if suitable filters have been installed.

To insert images from file:

Start from a blank slide, or from any other layout with a placeholder removed to make room.

Open the **Insert** menu, point to **Picture** and select **From File...**

Continue as in Publisher (see page 160).

10.8 Designs and Master Slides

There are four ways that you format your presentation as a set rather than as individual slides – through the Master Slide, the colour scheme, background or design template.

The Master Slide

The Master Slide sets the default design for the slides in your presentation (except the Title slide which has its own master). Unless you change them individually, the slides will use the colours and text formats set at this level. They will also display any images or footers that you insert into the Master Slide.

◆ Anything which you can do to an ordinary slide, e.g. insert an image, you can also do to a Master Slide – but it then affects the whole presentation.

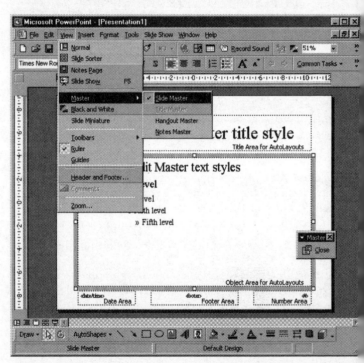

Figure 10.5 Editing the Master Slide to set text styles and any text or images to be shown on all slides.

To edit the Master Slide:

1 Open the **View** menu, point to **Master** and select **Slide Master**.

2 Select the title text or a bullet level.

3 Set the font, style, size and colour of the text.

4 If a logo or other image is wanted on all slides, insert it.

5 If you want to add a footer, click into the Footer area and type the text.

6 Click **Close** on the **Master** toolbar to return to Normal view.

Colour schemes

A scheme controls the colour of the background and of all the types of text. There are several predefined schemes to choose from, and you can define your own.

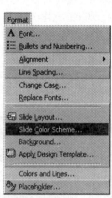

To apply a scheme:

1 Open the **Format** menu and select **Slide Color Scheme...**

2 At the **Color Scheme** dialog box, select a scheme and click **Preview** to see how it looks on your slide.

3 When you find a scheme you like, click **Apply to All** to apply it to all the slides in the presentation, or **Apply** to use it on the current slide only.

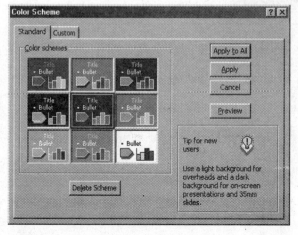

Background

The background colour or design can be set as part of a scheme or separately – and setting it separately gives you far more choice.

To format the background:

1 Open the **Format** menu and select **Background...**

2 At the **Background** dialog box, pick a colour from the small selection on the drop-down palette.

Or

3 Click **More Colors...** to define a new colour.

Or

4 Click **Fill Effects** to set a gradient, textured or pattern background. The options are exactly the same as for filled shapes (see page 193).

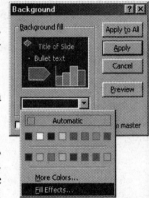

5 Click **Apply to All** to apply the background to all the slides in the presentation, or **Apply** to use it on the current slide only.

Picture backgrounds

If you want to use a picture as a background, go to the Picture tab of the Fill Effects dialog box and insert it from there. Take care with these – a picture only works as a background if the text is readable on top of it.

Design Templates

A design template has a background design, colour scheme and text styles. You can use one as a starting point for a new presentation or apply a template to an existing presentation.

To start from a design template:

1 Open the **File** menu and select **New**.

2 Go to the **Design Templates** tab of the **New Presentation** dialog box.

3 Pick a template and click **OK**.

To apply a design template to a presentation:

1 Open the **Format** menu and select **Apply Design Template...**

2 At the **Apply Design Template** dialog box, select a template – the preview pane will give you an idea of how it will look.

3 Scroll through until you find one you like, then click **Apply**.

The template will be applied to all the slides in the presentation.

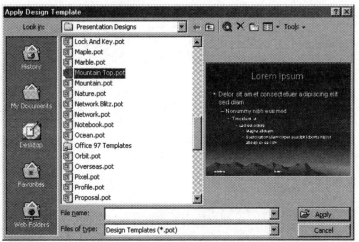

10.9 Templates and house styles

Many organizations have standard designs for their presentations, as they do for their stationery and other publications. It's partly about controlling the corporate image, and partly about ensuring consistent quality in their public output – just because someone is a good salesperson does not mean that he or she will be able to design a good-looking presentation.

To set up a house style, you need to create a template.

1 Start a new presentation – either from blank or from an existing design template.

2 Edit the Master Slide, adding the organization's name, logo and/or motto as required.

3 Open the **File** menu and select **Save As**.

4 At the **Save As** dialog box, select *Design Template (*.pot)* in the **Save as type** field.

5 Give the file a name to identify it clearly, and click **Save**.

10.10 Outlines and text levels

Outline view shows the structure of presentations more clearly, especially where they are text-based. The slide titles form the top level, with standard bullet lists making the second level of the structure. If there are bullets within bullets, these become the next lower level.

You can change the structure by moving text items up or down levels – promoting or demoting in PowerPoint jargon. If you demote a normal bullet point, it will become a second level bullet point; if you promote a normal bullet point, it becomes a slide title – on its own new slide!

To change text levels:

1 Switch to Outline view – this isn't essential but does show the text better than Normal view.

2 Select the line(s) of text.

3 Click ◀ to promote or ▶ to demote the text.

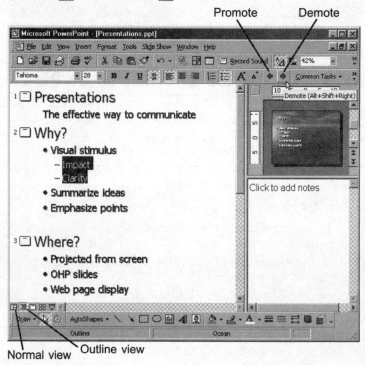

Normal view   Outline view

10.11 Previewing

If you are showing a presentation on screen, as 35mm slides, or through an overhead projector, the slides will look exactly the same as they did during construction. The printouts will also be almost identical from a colour printer. If you are printing on a black-only printer, use the **Black and White** view to check before printing. If images or backgrounds do not show well in the default black and white or *grayscale* (shades of grey), you can adjust their shading.

◆ These settings only affect the printouts. When you revert to a colour display, the slides will be unchanged.

To prepare for black and white printing:

1 Open the **View** menu and select **Black and White**.

2 Right-click on an image, or on the background, point to **Black and White** and select a Black, White or Grayscale option – repeat until you like what you see.

3 Select **View > Black and White** again to restore the colour on screen.

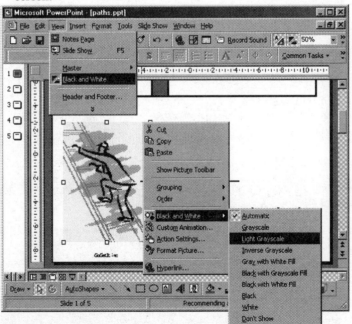

Figure 10.6 Some colour images come out poorly in black and white – you may prefer not to show these.

10.12 Printing

In PowerPoint you can print:

* the *slides*, as they appear on screen;
* the *notes*, by themselves;
* slides with accompanying notes as *handouts*;
* the text of the presentation, as an *outline*.

You can also select which slides to include and how many copies.

For a simple printout of all the slides (or to use the same settings as the last time you did a controlled print), just click the **Print** button 🖨. For anything else, use the menu command.

1 Open the **File** menu and select **Print**.
2 Set the **range** of slides to print.
3 Set the number of copies.
4 Select a **Print what** option – *Slides*, *Handouts*, *Notes Pages* or *Outline View*.
5 For Handouts, set the number per page.

You can select a different **Printer** – perhaps change to colour, instead of the default black and white?

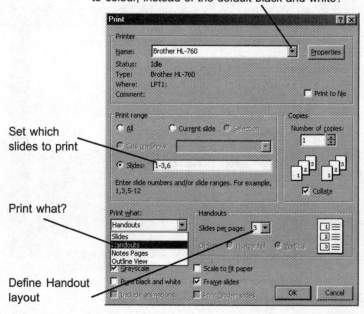

Set which slides to print

Print what?

Define Handout layout

6 Set the other options as required.

7 Click **OK**.

10.13 Running a slide show

For a simple slide show, switch to **Slide Show view** to start it running, then click the left button to bring up each slide in turn, and click again at the end to return to the PowerPoint window.

If you want to create a presentation that runs by itself, or that people can view by themselves, you need to do some preparation.

The Set Up Show dialog box

The main settings here are in the **Show type** and the **Advance slides** options.

- If you will be giving the presentation, select **Presented by a speaker** and set the advance to manual – unless you are very confident that you can deliver at the same speed as in rehearsal!

- If you want a self-running demonstration, use **Browsed at a kiosk** and timed advance.

- If you want people to control it themselves, select **Browsed by an individual** and manual advance.

1 Open the **Slide Show** menu and select **Set Up Show...**

2 Set the **Show type**.

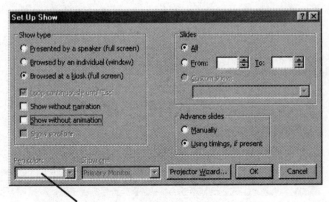

If you will be running the show, and drawing
on the screen, set the pen colour

3   For a partial show, set the **From:** and **To:** values, giving the slide numbers.

4   Set the **Advance slides** option.

5   Click **OK**.

Interactive presentations

If you right-click on the screen during a presentation, you will get these tools:

* **Next**, **Previous**, the **Go** options and **End Show** allow you to navigate freely through the show.

* The **Meeting Minder** lets you make notes and 'Action Items' as you present the show. These can all be called up from the **Tools** menu afterwards for reference, and – even better – the Action Items are automatically collated and dis-

played on a new slide at the end of the presentation.

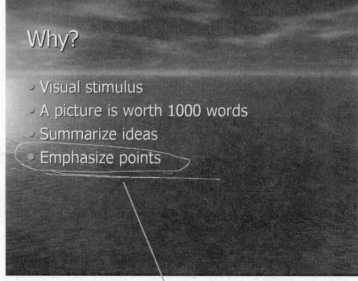

There's an art to drawing on screen with a mouse – and very few of us ever master it!

- **Speaker Notes** display any notes you added to a slide, in case you lose your way – and lose your printed notes!

- **Screen** lets you black out the display temporarily.

- **Pointer Options** allow you to hide the pointer, or switch to a pen so that you can draw on the screen to emphasize a point.

10.14 Exercise

Starting from a blank presentation or a design template, create a presentation to introduce a new product. Apart from the title slide, you will need slides which describe the product, outline the target market, give an overview of the advertising campaign.

Summary

- A presentation is a series of slides to be shown on screen or on an overhead projector.

- PowerPoint is the leading presentation software.

- New slides can be created quickly by starting from an AutoLayout.

- Text can only be created in text boxes or bulleted lists. It is edited and formatted in the same way as in Word.

- To create a slide containing clip art, start from an AutoLayout with a clip art placeholder. To add an image from file, use the Insert > Picture option.

- The Master Slide styles, colour schemes, background and design templates can all give more consistency to your presentations.

- You can adjust the structure of a presentation, and it is easiest to do this in Outline view.

- If you are printing in black and white, preview the slides to see how they will look, and adjust the colour if needed.

- You can run a slide show manually or set it up to run automatically.

Completing the New CLAIT course should have given you a good basic understanding of a range of computer applications and ICT activities, and the confidence to take it further. So where do you go from here?

OCR offer CLAIT Plus – a level 2 qualification – that builds directly on your New CLAIT skills. It is a set of individual units, including Microsoft Office Specialist ones, all of which lead to nationally recognised qualifications. They can be taken in any combination to suit your needs or interests. And you can go on from that to CLAIT Advanced, an NVQ Level 3 qualification.

CLAIT Plus and CLAIT Advanced are part of the OCR CLAIT Suite. You can find out more about the Suite at OCR's Web sites at **www.ocr.org.uk** and **www.clait.org.uk**.

If you do not want to go on to the next qualification, but would like to understand more about one or more of the applications and uses of ICT, there are *Teach Yourself* books on Windows, the Internet, HTML, Word, Excel, Access and PowerPoint.

The Internet is a very good resource for any aspect of ICT. For every application or topic, you will find at least one newsgroup where you can discuss common problems (and solutions). Microsoft, of course, has areas of its site devoted to each of its products, with frequently asked questions (FAQ) lists and other sources of help, but there are also plenty of sites run by user groups, publishers, training firms and enthusiasts, where you will find solutions and stimulus. They are easy to track down – just run a simple search for the application or topic at Google.

index

Excel 2002
moira stephen

- Are you new to Excel?
- Do you want help with many of the topics commonly found in exam syllabuses?
- Do you need lots of practice and examples to brush up your skills?

Excel 2002 is a comprehensive guide to this popular package and is suitable for all beginners. It progresses steadily from basic skills to more advanced features, with many time-saving shortcuts and practical advice.

Moira Stephen is a college lecturer and consultant trainer specializing in PC applications. She is the author of numerous computer books.

Word 2002
moira stephen

- Are you new to Word?
- Do you want help with many of the topics commonly found in exam syllabuses?
- Do you need lots of practice and examples to brush up your skills?

Word 2002 is a comprehensive guide to this word processing package and is suitable for beginners. The book progresses from basic skills to more advanced features, with many time-saving shortcuts. Its practical approach, numerous illustrations and guide to automating tasks make it an easy way to brush up your skills.

Moira Stephen is a college lecturer and consultant trainer specializing in PC applications. She is the author of numerous computer books.